Are You Still Watching?

Using Pop Culture to Tune In, Find God, and Get Renewed for Another Season

Are You Still Watching?

Using Pop Culture to Tune In, Find God, and Get Renewed for Another Season

Stephanie Kendell and
Arthur Stewart

Co-Hosts of the Two On One Project

**chalice
press**

Saint Louis, Missouri

An imprint of Christian Board of Publication

ChalicePress.com

Print: 9780827201064
EPUB: 9780827201071
EPDF: 9780827201088
Printed in Canada

We celebrate this book by saying...

"Happy Day, Alex and Davis!"

(Schitt's Creek S3:E13)

That is to say we are so grateful for everything and everyone that made this book possible: for all the days of celebration and the hard days we overcame, the days we unplugged to rest and the days we binged inspired stories, the days we learned to let go and the days that renewed us unexpectedly. We want to thank the people that continue to remind us that God is always present—we just have to tune in. Thank you to the streaming networks and media platforms that kept us engaged and connected when forced to be apart.

And finally, this book is dedicated to the people who renew us— our families, friends, Deuces, communities, and our expansive networks of support. You make the best days possible and our worst days bearable. Thank you for all the ways you tune in and keep watching our shared stories.

Contents

Introduction: Are You Still Watching?
The Reverend Stephanie Kendell and
The Reverend Arthur Stewart   *1*

Chapter One: Following a Gleaming Star: Epiphany,
Magi, and the Avett Brothers
The Reverend Daniel Lyvers   *7*

Chapter Two: Let Your Light Shine: Grief, Healing, and
Next to Normal
The Reverend Colton D. Lott   *15*

Chapter Three: Barbecue Sauce: *Ted Lasso,* Jesus, and
the Hermeneutic of Curiosity
The Reverend Stephanie Kendell   *25*

Chapter Four: Forget What's Behind: Sanctified
Imagination and *The Harder They Fall*
The Reverend Rae Karim   *37*

Chapter Five: Lord, Only You Can Answer That: Dry
Bones and *Get Back*
The Reverend Travis Smith McKee   *45*

Chapter Six: The Sun Has Gazed on Me: Song of Songs,
Beyoncé's *Black Parade* and Decolonization
The Reverend Larry J. Morris III   *55*

Chapter Seven: The Town Where I Currently Am: The
Kin-dom and *Schitt's Creek*
The Reverend Arthur Stewart   *65*

Chapter Eight: Do Our Choices Matter?
Free Will, Divine Order, and *Foundation*
The Reverend Jason Reynolds   75

Chapter Nine: One Body, Many Members:
Open Minds and *Queer Eye*
The Reverend Diane Faires Beadle   83

Chapter Ten: Where is Fat Jesus? Sympathizing in
Weakness and *My 600-lb Life*
The Reverend Doctor Delesslyn A. Kennebrew   91

Chapter Eleven: Go to Hell, Christian! The Afterlife,
This Life, and Netflix's *Lucifer*
The Reverend Shane Isner   99

Chapter Twelve: Chaos as Virtue: Lessons from *Loki*
on Mystery and Mischief
The Reverend Whitney Waller   111

Afterword: Keep Watching
The Reverend Arthur Stewart and
The Reverend Stephanie Kendell   121

Contributors   125

Endnotes   129

Are You Still Watching?

So, I say to you, ask, and it will be given you;
Search, and you will find;
Quarantine and eventually you will start a podcast.

In March 2020, when the world collectively shut down due to the global pandemic of the novel Coronavirus, many people of faith found themselves challenged with the new task of building meaningful and sustainable connections in a solely and suddenly digital world. Worship leaders rearranged their homes to stage makeshift pulpits and learned to use the small light of a camera as the fulcrum of connection with their congregants. Members of congregations were tasked with being the church while simultaneously being told to stay away from the church building. We were all challenged to look for God at work in new ways, all at home. This socially encapsulated existence became mundane quickly, and just as quickly, many of us turned to television, movies, books, music, and yes—even podcasts— to help us escape back into the world and the people we so desperately missed. And it did not take long before we were all asked, "Are you still watching?"

The first time you encounter an "Are You Still Watching?" it feels judgmental. We wanted to yell back, "Of course we are still watching! We can't go outside, and we need to know if Carol Baskin did it!" Days turned into months, episodes into seasons and spinoffs, and it was not long before we didn't even have to read the screen to know the question and unconsciously push the button on our pre-selected answer, "Keep watching."

And yet, an unexpected thing started to happen as we collectively binge-watched established and new shows alike. New glimmers of joy started to emerge from our collective streaming as old friends reconnected to talk about new shows, and we all started asking the question, "What's next?"

Over the months, the perfunctory question of, "Are You Still Watching?" moved from a judgmental question into a curious one—seemingly posed by a divine movement among us. "Are You Still Watching?" became a profound theological statement inviting us into deeper and more nuanced questions: Are you still paying attention to the world around you? Are you still connecting with the people you love? Are you still seeing the new things God is doing? These questions were placed against the backdrop of the solely digital church most of us were navigating at the time and the sense that momentum waned the longer we continued to be apart. Faith leaders, exhausted yet hopeful for something to renew their body and spirit, found that they, too, were asking their congregations the question that seemed to connect us all, "Are You Still Watching?" and then waiting to see if they would choose to keep going.

It was during that time that we, The Reverend Arthur Stewart and The Reverend Stephanie Kendell, also reconnected. We were peripheral friends—fond of one another, usually good for a birthday post on social media, and friendly, to be sure. One day, Arthur was doing a live feed on social media, and Stephanie (also known by the nickname "Spiff" to many) entered the chat. We talked for hours about what we were watching, TV characters we loved, movies we hated, and music we couldn't live without. We followed up the next week on another live show and talked about Stephen Sondheim's ninetieth birthday and our shared love of Sondheim's work and life. By the end of our time together, we had debated, laughed, and come to two very important conclusions: God was at work in pop culture, and our conversation had been fun!

The unexpected joy of our conversation brought a sense of renewal and energy for the wider work we are both called to do. That renewal, which for us often felt like new energy for old tasks and sustained excitement for those yet to be, quickly became a shared resource for our colleagues, especially those who struggled with finding new sources of inspiration. As faith leaders, we use the word renewal in the church often, but rarely do we explore the nuanced ways renewal looks for each of us. Who knew ours would come in the form of looking for God in the media we know and love, and then having a conversation about it with friends and colleagues around the world?

From those conversations, and with the encouragement and support of friends, family, and colleagues, the *Two On One Project* was born. Each week, the two of us have a dynamic, theological, and often spoiler-filled conversation with a guest about *one* aspect of pop culture. Now in our third season, we have interviewed some of the most notable and inspiring faith leaders working for the church today. We and our Deuces (*Two On One Project* listeners) have experienced renewal through unexpected joy, beloved community, vulnerable connection, and a shared belief that *Love Actually* is an awful movie.

The necessity of our new digital reality in the church highlighted just how important community is to our faith, our mental health, and our ability to care for each other. The Bethany Fellows, a ministry organization that serves congregations by assisting newly ordained pastors' transition from seminary to sustained congregational ministry, knew that since the church was changing, so would the way Bethany Fellows helped congregations. While none of us have pastored through a global pandemic before, the Bethany Fellows worked to answer the question we were all too afraid to ask, "Will we be renewed?"

Luckily, both of us are Bethany Fellows and have been the recipients of their incredible support. *Two On One Project* would not be here without Bethany Fellows, as we—not just Stephanie and Arthur, but all our contributing authors—are either past or present Fellows and had access to the tools and networks of support created by Bethany Fellows to navigate this unknown time. This book is brought to you in partnership with The Bethany Fellows and Chalice Press. The Bethany Fellows' commitment to congregational care is part of why this book is meant to be a resource for congregations and their leaders for tuning in, finding God, and getting renewed for another season of life and ministry.

On *Two On One Project*, we end each episode by asking our guests, "What biblical character, book, verse, or theme are you most reminded of in our pop culture topic?" Our question is an invitation to our guests each week and to you, dear readers, to tune in and find God in new places, like a dart game in a small English pub or the harmonies of a Broadway musical. We hope this new connection with God will offer you some much-needed rest and renewal from the challenging work of being human in a very human world. The divine spark is everywhere if we seek it. Yes, even in hip-hop and country music, even in streaming television shows and blockbuster movies. Our faith is a story—we hear the stories, we learn the stories, we tell the stories—and believe us, God is in every one of these stories.

So, we hope that the stories you read here, stories of how God speaks through pop culture, will inspire you to try a French tuck and seek the Divine in places you may have overlooked. We hope you will come to know that there is a difference between just listening and fully experiencing the Holy Spirit in Beyoncé and to realize that it is okay if the Avett Brothers is your hymnal. Finally, we hope you feel connected to a group of people who also feel that some days a well-placed "Ew, David" sounds an awful lot like an "Amen."

In short, we hope this book helps you and your congregation to always hit "Keep Watching" when God asks, "Are You Still Watching?" (Because we all know this connection is the only way we will get renewed for Season 2 and beyond).

Two On One Project is a spoilers show, and this book is no exception. This book—which, again, *contains spoilers* to the media it engages—has been structured to facilitate a year-long study, using one chapter each month. It can be transposed into a weekly series, too—you bought the book (thank you!), so please use it as you need. In the table of contents and title of each essay, you will find the cultural touchstones our authors used in conversation with biblical texts and themes. You may want to engage these touchstones before you read the chapter. Once you have read the chapter, we offer reflective questions meant to help you think expansively about the topic and themes therein. This book does have an intentional design moving you through the calendar with each chapter, though each chapter can also stand alone. However, if you were to start at the beginning of the calendar year, being mindful of the liturgical calendar as well, you'll see our intentions.

Daniel Lyvers begins our year at the Epiphany, in *Follow a Gleaming Star*, talking about the magi, the Avett Brothers, and what it means to be open to what comes next. As the days get longer, **Colton Lott** writes about how *We Need Some Light*, asking faithful questions about discipleship, mental health, and family. For the season of Lent, **Stephanie Kendell** examines the hermeneutic of curiosity and how we might seek a deeper Jesus in *Barbecue Sauce*. **Rae Karim** offers a Holy Week meditation on vengeance, remembering, and forgetting in *Forget What's Behind*. In Eastertide, **Travis Smith-McKee** holds both what was and what might be in *Lord, Only You Can Answer That.* As we enter ordinary time, which is anything but ordinary, we engage the holy day of Juneteenth and the strength of one's identity with **Larry Morris III**'s *The Sun Has Gazed On Me.* We continue the season with **Arthur Stewart** as he writes about the kin-dom of God and community in *The Town In Which I Currently Am*, and as we move into the next season of life, **Jason Reynolds** asks, *Do Our Choices Really Matter?* and holds in tension the gift of free will within the structure of predestination. As we continue toward the last third of the essays and possibly even the year, **Diane Faires Beadle** considers what happens if the church really means *everybody* when we say all are welcome in *One Body, Many Members.* For World Communion Sunday, **Delesslyn Kennebrew** asks, *Where is Fat Jesus?* at our tables and how self-love leads to a deeper connection to Christ. We close out the Christian year and this book with themes of the known and unknown with **Shane Isner's** *Go to Hell, Christian!*, and finally, we look to a hectic and beautiful season of Advent with **Whitney Waller's** *Chaos as Virtue.*

Again, dear readers, dear Deuces, and dear new friends, we know that these last few years have been both a gift and a challenge (and let's be honest, the latter is much more easily identifiable), but through the *Two On One Project* and the essays you are about to engage with, we hope that you too will be inspired to tune in, find God, and get renewed for another season of life, ministry, and community. These last few years have given us more questions than answers, but what we do know is this: God is still watching, and we hope you are too.

"'You miss 100% of the shots you don't take.
    —Wayne Gretzky'
        —Michael Scott."[1]
            —*Two On One Project* Arthur and Stephanie

Chapter One

Following a Gleaming Star: Epiphany, Magi, and the Avett Brothers

The Reverend Daniel Lyvers

The band The Avett Brothers has a three-part series of albums called "The Gleam." The original *The Gleam* was released in 2006, *The Second Gleam* in 2008, and the most recent, *The Third Gleam*, came out in August 2020. A lot of life happens in fourteen years, and still there are themes that weave this series, and arguably the full musical catalog of The Avett Brothers, together. Seth Avett, the younger Avett brother and the one that usually plays the guitar, describes *The Third Gleam* as:

> ...the sound of my brother and I in a room, singing about what is on our minds and in our hearts at the time... sharing it now is about what sharing art is always about: another chance that we may partake in connecting with our brothers and sisters of this world, and hopefully

joining you in noticing a speck of light gleaming in what
appears to be a relatively long and dark night.[2]

The Avett Brothers are a band from Concord, North Carolina.
There are two brothers, Scott and Seth Avett; and a bassist, Bob
Crawford, that joined them in the very early days. Bob booked
their first tour and nudged them to take their music to the world.
Then, fan favorite cellist Joe Kwon began playing with them in
2007 and has made himself indispensable ever since.[3]

Their musical genre is tricky to define. There's a banjo, a guitar,
a bass, and then...a cello, keyboards, drums, an occasional organ,
and those sweet vocal harmonies. The guitar is sometimes
electric, while the vocals are country and twangy in one song
and punk rock-ish in the next.

Some may call The Avett Brothers' music folk, some rock, others
a mashup known as folk-rock. Others have tried the labels
Americana, bluegrass, or country. However you define the genre
in musical terms, The Avett Brothers have played together for
over twenty years, so their sound reflects the passage of time and
the growth of a band constantly discovering its music together.

For me, I describe their music as authentic, tender, vulnerable,
and human. Ultimately, The Avett Brothers have written
and performed music that speaks to the messy, bizarre,
wonderfully holy, and complex experience of being human.
They present songs of process, of journeys of trial and error,
and of experiencing deep love and real heartbreak. There's a
rhythm of faithfulness and openness, and of going one direction
and then having to change direction. There's wisdom, folly, and
vanity. To listen to the Avetts is to be let into the deepest parts
of their journey, a search for meaning and purpose in a world
of uncertainty.

The Avett Brothers offer music for when it's "sometimes hard to
see love in anything," and it encourages listeners to "step back

into the light"[4] and look toward that gleaming speck begging us to notice it.

Themes in their music include openness, following a light to an uncertain path, and going one direction and changing somewhere along the way. Kind of magi-like, right?

Barbara Brown Taylor writes, "The Story of the Magi ranks right up there with the Christmas and Easter stories in terms of snaring the human imagination."[5] I'd guess many of us church folks are familiar with the story of Epiphany and the magi. There are songs about three kings traversing afar. Nativity sets are often adorned with "wise men" carrying gifts of gold, frankincense, and myrrh. Then there's that star.

As often is the case, the more a story is told, the more it takes on details that are not actually there. Matthew's gospel never says the "wise men" are kings, nor does Matthew specify three of them. As Amy-Jill Levine argues, "given Matthew's view of kings, to call the magi 'kings' would be odd. Nor would any early reader of Matthew's Gospel see the magi as kings."[6] The thought that there were three of them comes from the reference to the three gifts they bring. Levine writes, "There may have been seven Magi, or ten, or more,"[7] and likely, they probably were not all men.

The importance of the magi is their presence, a tone-setting moment in the beginning of Matthew's gospel that tells the reader of the expansiveness of the good news that will unfold in the story. Additionally, the significance of the magi is in their actions, both in following a star and in denying Herod's orders by not returning to him and instead going home "by another road" (Mt. 2:12).

And what about that star? According to Matthew, the star was the guide that led the magi to Jesus, Mary, and Joseph (Mt. 2:9). There have been many articles attempting to explain the star of

Bethlehem scientifically. Perhaps it was a planetary conjunction, like in December 2020, when Jupiter and Saturn appeared closer together than they had in centuries, thus showing up as a mesmerizing dot of bright light in the sky.[8]

Yet these attempts to explain the star miss the point. As Amy-Jill Levine puts it, "The star of Bethlehem is not about science, it is about the search for meaning."[9]

These stories that make up our faith tradition should be stories that open our imagination. They are stories that don't need to be easily explained or passed off as science or history lessons. Like a star that dots the night sky, these stories should catch our attention and make us wonder: *What is God up to?*

That is what epiphany moments do, after all: catch our attention, stop us in our tracks, and nudge us to enter the rhythm of movement that is God's creative flow. The story of the magi is an invitation to its readers to foster wonder and an attentiveness to the surprising, holy ways God disrupts us.

I wonder about the star that the magi saw. Was it a blinding light, or was it just reflective enough to make them notice, a gleam that made them stop and say, "Maybe I ought to explore that a little further"?

From the beginning of Matthew's gospel are clues for the reader about what entering this unfolding story will entail. It is a story of openness, journey, courage, risk, transformation, and a search for meaning.

These are the same themes that so consistently define the music of The Avett Brothers.

The first time I was introduced to their music was the summer after my first year of college. Fittingly, I was on the road, driving back from a week of counseling camp, when my friend said, "Here's a band you might like." He played me two songs.

The first was "Laundry Room," a song about being young and in love, with lyrics about wishing on shooting stars and the nostalgia that accompanies being human. We are "breathing time machines," after all.[10]

The other song was "Murder in the City," which contains my favorite lyric they've ever written: "Always remember there is nothing worth sharing like the love that lets us share our name."[11] Having originally written it to speak of the love between family, Scott Avett, the older Avett brother on the banjo, now says that each time he sings those words, he thinks of our collective, shared name: human.[12]

After hearing those songs in the car that day, I went home and immediately downloaded every album they had available. What followed has felt like my own journey of self-discovery shared alongside theirs, which feels appropriate since faith is often explored in community. Their music gives voice to emotions I can't adequately express for myself; their lyrics help me feel deeply and prompt epiphanies of my own.

The Avett Brothers' music is raw and tender, rooted in themes of human experience, such as the search for meaning, discernment of what it means to live and be alive in this world, and remembering that the journey of life and faith is a shared one. In their song "The Once and Future Carpenter," they sing, "Now I spend my days in search of a woman we call purpose, and if I ever pass back through her town I'll stay," before returning to a chorus that says:

Forever I will move like the world
that turns beneath me
And when I lose my direction, I'll look up to the sky
And when the black dress drags upon the ground
I'll be ready to surrender, and remember
We're all in this together
If I live the life I'm given, I won't be scared to die.[13]

These are lyrics that speak to the reality of life. We move, we get lost, we look for something that gives us direction, and ultimately, we live into all of it, knowing we're not alone and that who we are is more than enough to give us courage for the way.

The Avett Brothers are not unfamiliar with the Herods among us, and their music doesn't avoid that confrontation. I can imagine the magi singing along to the words of "Salvation Song." As the banjo strums in their heads and they go home by another way, I imagine them humming:

> We came for salvation
> We came for family
> We came for all that's good that's how we'll
> walk away
> We came to break the bad
> We came to cheer the sad
> We came to leave behind the world a better way
> ...and if it compromises truth than we will go.[14]

These words so simply capture much of the journey of faithfulness, yet to live in such a way is not always so simple. To come for salvation, good, and joy puts us right in the face of injustice, evil, and grief. That is where the star leads, though— where love takes on flesh and salvation takes root: in the midst of the heartbreak and hurt. We hear the invitation to come while knowing that, at points, we will be asked to compromise those holy truths and turn around.

The Avett Brothers' music is written through living it. They attest to that in reflecting on their song "No Hard Feelings" as a song that is particularly vulnerable because it took the most living to write.[15] It's music that roots us in an embodied faith. To know the gospel stories, to know love and hope, we have to live it. Not perfectly, yet actively. I find comfort as the Avetts sing, "regret for every step I took from Fisher Road to Hollywood. Feeling bad and acting good, never was content...but still I had to go."[16] It's a song of journey filled with wrong turns and moments of discernment. So often, epiphany experiences make very little sense, and yet still we have to go.

There's wisdom in the music of The Avett Brothers. One might even call them...wise men. However, as with the magi in Matthew, wisdom does not equal perfection. Wisdom is noticing, going, not compromising truth, changing direction when you need to, and taking the risk to follow the star, even if the end destination is uncertain.

From The Avett Brothers and the magi, we learn that faithfulness is a movement, a story that is experienced; and regardless of the roundabout way it takes us to get there, it somehow leads to the surprising presence of love in flesh.

Music, art, and the literary masterpieces that are the gospels connect us with the holy in incredible ways. At this moment, I hear this invitation: follow the *gleaming* star. Epiphanies are not often earth-shattering revelations but specks of light that spark curiosity. Epiphanies invite us to lean into wonder and imagination. Yes, it is dangerous and risky and undoubtedly leads to getting lost and starting over. But at this point on the way, perhaps we can find an additional compass from the music of The Avett Brothers:

Yes, we live uncertainty
And disappointments have to be
And every day we might be facing more
And yes, we live in desperate times
But fading words and shaking rhymes
There's only one thing here worth hoping for
With Lucifer beneath you and God above
If either one of them asks you what your living of
Say love...[17]

Reflection Questions:

- What are your "gleam moments"—experiences that caught your attention and changed your direction?

- Who are the musicians, poets, or artists that help give voice to human experience for you and connect you to the sacred?

- What are your North Stars, the compasses that you use to guide you along the way?

- Pick a song from the Avett Epiphany playlist and listen to it. What lyrics, themes, or thoughts stand out, and how do they speak to your understanding of faith?

- What do the magi represent for you, and who are your "modern-day magi?"

The Avett Brothers' Epiphany Playlist:
- Back Into the Light—Album: *The Third Gleam*

- Laundry Room—Album: *I and Love and You*

- Murder in the City—Album: *The Second Gleam*

- The Once and Future Carpenter—Album: *The Carpenter*

- Salvation Song—Album: *Mignonette*

- No Hard Feelings—Album: *True Sadness*

- Fisher Road to Hollywood—Album: *True Sadness*

- Living of Love—Album: *Emotionalism*

- Head Full of Doubt/Road Full of Promise—Album: *I and Love and You*

- Backwards with Time—Album: *The Gleam*

Chapter Two

Let Your Light Shine: Grief, Healing, and *Next to Normal*

The Reverend Colton D. Lott

I'm a sucker for stories about dysfunctional families, especially the (abundant) subtype of dead or compromised mothers. *Billy Elliot,* with a maternal-sized hole in his heart, always makes me cry. *August: Osage County,* with addicted and ailing Violet, jolts me with understanding. I feel drawn to these stories because they confront the deep pain that can come in family life; and in that process, I find recognition.[18]

My mother died from alcoholism when I was sixteen. It is a *complex* grief, where deep sadness is mingled with anger, relief, and sometimes an embarrassing joy. I call this grief complex, not only because of the multiple emotions, but because it is *sticky,* lingering and impacting multiple seasons of my life. More than a decade later, I can still transport myself to the quiet Saturday morning with my paternal grandmother, where I simply asked as she hung up the telephone, "Mom's dead, isn't she?" She nodded back yes, her eyes brimming with tears.

Until my congregation did a worship series on mental illness in the fall of 2021, I never fully realized that my life has been profoundly touched by mental illness. Despite my own time spent in psychotherapy—and psychology and pastoral care coursework in both undergrad and graduate school—I didn't recognize my mother's alcoholism as a mental illness. Only recently have I begun to use this language to describe the complex grief I carry.[19]

Along this journey of discovery, *Next to Normal* is a work of art that has accompanied me for the last decade. Written by Tom Kitt and Brian Yorkey, *Next to Normal* is the 2009 Pulitzer Prize-winning Broadway musical that tells the story of one woman, Diana, who has a mental illness, and how it impacts her and her family.

It's my favorite musical—especially because it tells the truth about how hard it can be to live in relation to a mental illness, which often casts metaphorical, yet nonetheless stifling, shadows. But more than simply telling the truth with beauty, *Next to Normal* has something to teach the church and those who follow Jesus. It has something to teach us about what it means to live vulnerably and honestly so that we might live rightly before God and with each other—and ultimately let our lights shine.

What drew me to *Next to Normal* is that it tells the story of a family with its own complex grief that resonated with my own. The Goodman family is attempting to be perfectly normal, to be notable only insofar as they are unnoteworthy. As the first lines of the sung-through musical begin, Diana Goodman, the protagonist, sings:

> They're the perfect, loving family, so adoring.
> And I love them every day of every week.
> So, my son's a little shit, my husband's boring.
> And my daughter, though a genius, is a freak.[20]

As we acclimate to their suburban world, it becomes predictably clear that they are, in fact, not a perfect family. Natalie, the daughter, is burning out as a high school student and piano prodigy. Dan, the husband, is drowning under the weight of pretenses and trying to keep Diana healthy, even to the detriment of his own health and happiness. And the son is dead. Despite seeming like an embodied, living, teenaged young man in the first half of Act I, we learn that he has been dead "sixteen years."[21] He is one of Diana's delusions, and only her character can see and interact with him.

The audience quickly learns that Diana has "bipolar [disorder]... with delusional episodes."[22] The story turns on this chapter of the family's experience of mental illness, filtered and affected by the complex grief that accompanies the death of a young child. Diana's inability to say goodbye to the son she lost sixteen years prior mingles with Dan's unwillingness to acknowledge any loss at all, even going so far as to refuse to speak his son's name. Natalie, feeling like "the invisible girl," ultimately attempts to cope by raiding her mother's medication, using drugs, and denying herself a romantic relationship with her boyfriend.[23]

Despite their attempts to be perfectly normal, the effects of mental illness mean that the life the Goodman family dreams of and idolizes is beyond their grasp.

Unlike the comfort I find in theater focusing on dysfunctional families, the Sermon on the Mount haunts me. Found in Matthew 5–7, the Sermon on the Mount is a manifesto from Jesus about what life should look like if it is lived rightly before God and with each other.[24] In it, Jesus describes a life lived with a rigorous ethic.

The Sermon on the Mount is wide ranging. After beginning with upside-down (or right-side-up) blessings (often called the beatitudes), the sermon takes off with Jesus' thoughts on anger, adultery, divorce, oaths, retaliation, and love for enemies.

It details the proper way to give alms (secretly), pray (in this way), fast (without looking dismal), and store up treasures (don't). The command to not worry, alongside the golden rule, "do to others as you would have them do to you" (Mt. 7:12), is also contained in the sermon. Jesus ends with a short parable of "the wise man who built his house on rock" in contrast to the "foolish [man] who built his house on sand" and the summation that we should not just hear these words of Jesus and but also "act on them" (Mt. 7:24).

I say that the sermon haunts me because the bar Jesus sets doesn't just seem high—it seems impossibly, unreachably high. As a leader and teacher in the church, one line from Jesus is especially sobering. He says:

> Whoever breaks one of the least of these commandments, **and teaches others to do the same**, will be called least in the [kin-dom] of heaven.
> (Mt. 5:19 **emphasis mine**)

There are many mysteries of the Christian faith, but one of them that seems less mysterious to me is that I do not want to be *least* in the family of God. Nevertheless, I teach and preach before dozens of people in any given week, and despite Jesus being vast in his ethics, it is in the particulars where I, and the people I know and love, get stuck.

We might give alms secretly, but how much is right when a parent is pinching pennies between paychecks? We might seek reconciliation, but what if the conflict in question was caused by bodily harm or assault, and to go and "come to terms quickly with your accuser" (Mt. 5:25a) causes more trauma and unjustly burdens the victim by requiring them to come into proximity with the perpetrator? We might want to forsake all treasure hoarding on earth, but does a 401(k) count as a necessity for living in an industrialized world with the notion of a retirement? Or is it simply sin?

When I follow the anxiety spiral that can accompany the Sermon on the Mount, scared by the consequences of teaching the wrong things, I can easily find myself in a similar boat to the Goodman family in *Next to Normal*. The gap between the ideal and real is not a fissure but a chasm; life, filled with things like complex grief, does not square neatly with our desires or plans.

My first impulse when I experience the Sermon on the Mount is to desire perfection and normalcy. More precisely, I want to be perfectly normal—a perfectly normal follower of Jesus, who checks all the boxes, fits in all the schemes, and is noteworthy only insofar as I am unnoteworthy.

I just want to get it right instead of wrong. But that ideal isn't possible. And if the Sermon on the Mount is only about fulfilling some unattainable perfection, then I have already failed.

Toward the beginning of the sermon is a command from Jesus to "[let] your light shine before others, so that they may see your good works and give glory to your [God] in heaven" (Mt. 5:16b).

This is a curious command because our light has to shine *so that* our good works, our adherence to this ethic of Jesus, can be seen. This "shining of light" seems to even precede and accompany the good works, rather than being a byproduct of right living. Perhaps this notion of shining light could be a key that helps this text of Jesus come alive in liberation, instead of being a weight that keeps us from finding wholeness of life. Similarly, *Next to Normal* teaches me something important about how we let our light shine and live our lives before God and with others, even as we exist in the messy middle of life.

Throughout *Next to Normal*, the Goodman family runs the gauntlet in trying to address the mental illness at the center of their lives. Through the course of Act I, Diana cycles through a variety of interventions: psychopharmaceuticals, talk therapy without medication, and finally electroconvulsive therapy (ECT), which causes her to have profound memory loss and disorientation in Act II. Natalie is consumed with drugs and closes herself off from her boyfriend. Dan becomes mentally abusive as he manipulates the loss and disorientation Diana experiences after ECT to give her a life that is "better than before," a life which notably does not include memories or references to their dead son.[25] But the memories slowly return, and a conflict within the couple returns Diana to her psychiatrist's office, where she finally decides to forego any further psychiatric or psychotherapeutic intervention.[26]

At this emotional moment, the musical climaxes, and Diana and Natalie are finally able to speak honestly to one another in the song "Maybe (Next to Normal)." Diana promises Natalie that,

"Things will get better, you'll see."[27] To which Natalie replies, "Not for me."[28]

After they go back and forth for a few lines between Diana's optimism and Natalie's pessimism, Diana offers instead:

Maybe we can't be okay
But maybe we're tough, and we'll try anyway.
We'll live with what's real. Let go of what's past.
And maybe I'll see you at last.
We tried to give you a normal life.
I realize now, I have no clue what that is.[29]

Natalie sings back the truth as she knows it:

I don't need a life that's normal.
That's way too far away.
But something next to normal would be okay.[30]
With this new honesty, the idolized ideals are
washed away.

Instead, the mother and daughter choose vulnerability and speak the truth. They can recognize the realities that come with being a child loving a parent who has a mental illness or being a parent loving a child while also having a mental illness.

When we are vulnerable with each other, we can finally tell the truth. Normalcy is impossible to reach; perfection doesn't exist! Checking all the boxes is an impossible task. Being noteworthy for being unnoteworthy is a dream. Simply being "right" or "perfectly normal" cannot happen. Our lives are marked by complex grief. Chasing some idolized ideal doesn't lead to a goodness that shines.

Paradoxically, when we tell the truth about all the things we fear might dim our light—our griefs, failings, and faults—our light shines. Instead of glossing over the difficult parts of life and pretending everything is "normal," another way becomes possible. Perhaps this is what letting our light shine before God and others might mean: living with vulnerability to tell the truth as we know it, and then trying to do the best with what we have and who we are.

One of the thematic elements of *Next to Normal* is, coincidentally, light. The show first begins with Diana sitting in darkness. At the close of Act I, Dan asks Diana to undergo ECT because it is "a light in the dark."[31] At the end of Act II, we turn to Dan sitting in the dark, Diana having left him to discover healing on her own. He is crying as he finally grapples with his own long-suppressed, complex grief around his deceased son. Natalie enters the scene and finds her father here. She tells him, "[We] need some light."[32]

In the show's denouement, the family begins living in that light and simultaneously begins their healing journeys by practicing vulnerability, honesty, and receiving the support they need.

In the last lines of the show, the cast sings out:

> When we open up our lives,
> Sons and daughters,
> Husbands, wives

Can fight that fight.
There will be light.[33]

Even though it is not always how I want wholeness and right living before God and with others to look, opening up my own life in vulnerability and courage is the path to letting my light shine. While it might seem easier to avoid the pain in my family, living honestly is the only way I know how to live as a follower of Jesus, which includes all of me and thus lets *my* light shine through. Perhaps this is true for you, too.

Letting our light shine through us with a vulnerability that begets honesty won't be a cure-all. But I believe that shining our light creates a way to begin our own healing and to find ways to live rightly before God, with others, and even with ourselves. While the presence of vulnerability and honesty does not mean that we have figured out how to live, it gives us an actual start. Rather than imagining that the high standard Jesus invites us to in the Sermon on the Mount is merely an exam to fail, we can instead claim it as the communal hope of living better together. We claim it in hope, not despite our perfection, but precisely because we recognize that much of life rests in the muck and mire of hurts, illnesses, addictions, and woes. Jesus gives us the chance to do right by one another, but only if we start with the truth as we know it. We must begin our attempt at right living before God and with others with honest light, instead of trying to begin from the idol of normalcy.

This way of living is a risky proposition that rests on a "maybe." But letting my light shine so that we might shine together is a chance important enough for me to take.

May my light shine. May your light shine, too. And even if we're next to normal, at least we are no longer deluded by the idol of "perfectly normal" or "notably unnoteworthy." Instead, we might be known as a people of love, of works made good because of our vulnerability and honesty, because we first let our light shine.

Reflection Questions:

- Do you carry a complex grief? What might it mean for you to share that grief with others?

- How do you feel about the Sermon on the Mount? Is it a guide, an ideal, an impossible standard, a group project, rules and regulations, or something else?

- What works of art have resonated with your experience of grief, loss, or illness? Did they transform the way you thought of God, faith, or your Christian practices?

- Where have you witnessed healing after vulnerable honesty?

- If you were to start with the vulnerability that begets honesty and let your light shine, what part of your life would you begin with? What do you think might happen next?

Chapter Three

Barbeque Sauce: Ted Lasso, Jesus, and the Hermeneutic of Curiosity

The Reverend Stephanie Kendell

The Prince's Head pub is the central gathering place in town, away from the field, locker room, and front office, where everyone—fans, coaches, owners, and onlookers alike—celebrate, lament, and discuss their beloved football club, AFC Richmond. It's noticeably tense inside. Coach Ted Lasso, the American football coach recently hired to lead AFC Richmond, has challenged Rupert, the club's former owner, to a game of darts. The wager is large; if Rupert wins, he sets the starting lineup for AFC Richmond in the last two games of the season, effectively shutting out Coach Lasso from the job he was called to do. The scoreboard says "Rupert" on one side and "Wanker" on the other, a clear sign of the crowd's allegiance. The game is close as they enter the final throw. Coach Lasso needs to throw a seemingly impossible round to win. With his friends, fans, and even betrayer huddled close to watch what happens, he pauses and reflects:

> You know, Rupert, guys have underestimated me my entire life. And for years, I never understood why. It used to really bother me. But then one day, I was driving my little boy to school, and I saw this quote by Walt Whitman, and it was painted on the wall there. It said, "Be curious, not judgmental." I like that.

Ted throws his first dart right on target as the crowd cheers.

> So, I get back in my car and I'm driving to work, and all of a sudden it hits me. All them fellas that used to belittle me, not a single one of them were curious. You know, they thought they had everything all figured out. So, they judged everything, and they judged everyone. And I realized that they're underestimating me...who I was had nothing to do with it. 'Cause if they were curious, they would've asked questions. You know? Questions like, "Have you played a lot of darts, Ted?"

Ted throws his second dart which lands squarely on target.

> To which I would've answered, "Yes, sir. Every Sunday afternoon at a sports bar with my father, from age ten till I was sixteen, when he passed away."...Barbecue sauce.[34]

Ted throws the final dart, and it is a bullseye...

A man travels far from home to expand on his gifts and what he feels called to do in this world: coach, teach, help, and lead. To some, it may look like authoritative work; getting to say who is in and who is out is often the work of the one in charge, the one casting the vision for what comes next. But this man has always been more of a team player. All we (his fans and followers) can do now is have faith that if we follow his lead, he will lead us to victory.

He is a stranger in a strange land, and he does not have an insider's perspective on customs, foods, languages, and ways of being. Our confidence in him is not guaranteed but earned. Yet there is an air of trust that is building above the low hum of dissent from the wider community. We know who he is right from the beginning when we were given his resume. Every part of the story in which we fear the worst for him—and therefore, for us—he shows up with vision and hope. He is consistent. He has known from the beginning that this was about the journey, not the destination; all he needs now is to know that we aren't *just* fans but participants, each called to do our part to the best of our abilities for communal success. Our individual job descriptions may vary, but at the heart of it all, his leadership requires us to put in the hard work of being present with each other and helping the team succeed in every season. Even in seasons of certainty, where the win or the loss seems inevitable, he reminds us to be curious, not judgmental. And so Jesus asks:

> "Who do people say that the Son of Man is?" And [the disciples] said, "Some say John the Baptist, but others Elijah, and still others Jeremiah or one of the prophets." He said to them, "But who do you say that I am?" Simon Peter answered, "You are the Messiah, the Son of the living God." (Mt. 16:13–16, NRSV)

We are all born into traditions. Some traditions are celebrated and shared, while others we help end for a myriad of reasons. But nonetheless, all traditions inform our future generations. In church, it is not uncommon to hear stories about the place where family and faith traditions merge. Sayings like "I was raised in this church" tell us something about both the family and the faith community. I, however, was neither born into a faith tradition nor raised in the church. I was born into the tradition of team sports and have been a faithful follower ever since.

In August of 2020, when Apple TV+ released *Ted Lasso*, everyone tuned in to see how Coach Lasso would navigate his new world. Twitter exploded with quotes and memes, Halloween costumes of the cast were inevitable and unavoidable, and suddenly people who had never been interested in sports found themselves actively participating in a soccer fan base with opinions on players, coaches, and a winning strategy. While these conversations were happening everywhere, Coach Lasso's leadership posture of curiosity seemed to especially resonate with people in faith communities. In a tradition that has relied heavily on certainty through statements of faith, doctrines, and creeds, Coach Lasso's operating ethic—summed up in Season 1 Episode 8 as, "Be curious, not judgmental,"[35] which I have named as the hermeneutic of curiosity—seemed to resonate deeply with people as a way to posture themselves toward growth in their faith development, communal care, and hospitality.

As we tuned into each episode, suddenly we as people of faith were not seeing a soccer team fight against relegation but rather a congregation struggling to keep up with the changing times. We could all name the Jamies in our community—the young people we prayed for who have abundant gifts to share and strengthen our community, but whose passions, clothes, language, and focus challenge the institution. So we hold them back until they learn to pass the ball better and become more like us; but often, they just find another team. Or the Rebeccas— strong women we have been told to fear or to silence because they don't fit into the role the church has defined for them. And the church is ripe with Roys—established members with recognized ways of doing things who are often hesitant to affirm anything new, but who have the earned authority to effect big change within the community.

Each *Ted Lasso* episode turned our altars into grassy fields and our congregants into a team full of players. We felt each win—a new gift, a new member, a new ministry—and yet relegation still looms in the not-too-distant future. So we turn to our coach, hoping there is a solution. Maybe a trick play will bring about immediate success. And while Coach loves a good set piece, he knows a fast and quick goal won't actually address a team's brokenness. We are certain we have all the tools we need. We have all the right players, we practice, we even put money into the field; none of the *things* for success are missing. But that is why we have Coach, a person whose vision is communal and whose authority is shared with the team captain and kit man alike. Coach appreciates but isn't invested in the short game. He has a plan, but it's a strategy that takes intention and commitment. We are playing to win the season, not just the game. So we need to keep asking, "Who do you say that I am?" (Mt. 16:15) And maybe more importantly, who do we say that *we* are? That is the coach's long game. And there is one proven and effective strategy...

Curiosity.

Curiosity is how we move forward. That's how we heal a broken team. That is how we win.[36]

Certainty in Christ may be the destination, the big W of salvation some people want, but curiosity is the journey Jesus requires of us. The journey he not only models for us but accompanies us on. Jesus knows that curiosity is the real name of the game. Winning was never about the number of goals in the net or people in the pews, but how we work together as a team and how we treat the players on the other teams too. Or as Coach Lasso says:

> For me, success is not about the wins and losses. It's about helping these young fellas be the best versions of themselves on and off the field. And it ain't always easy... but neither is growing up without someone believing in you.[37]

Coach Lasso's hermeneutic of curiosity helps us remember that there is always more than what we know. His curiosity models for the church a way we, too, can show our belief in another's abilities and support the ways God is at work in their life. The hermeneutic of curiosity opens up a team roster for gifts we didn't know we needed, and it helps a church community find God in new ways, by naming the gifts in someone that have traditionally gone unnamed or unseen.

For example, what might a church gain in their relationship with God if they asked a Jamie in their community to teach Bible Study? What if the unique way "Jamie" exists in this world is an interpretive lens for the text that their community hasn't experienced before? What would you discover if you asked the Rebeccas, who have untapped leadership gifts in abundance, what God is calling them to in the life of the church and what might it look like for the community to support that ministry? And what might happen if we ask the Roys to rest for a moment, so that another player like Sam or Dani, with a full tank of energy, might help the team in a new way? How might that rest renew the Roys for the games and season ahead? How might being curious about individuals shift the team dynamic in ways that renew rather than relegate? Ted Lasso's hermeneutic of curiosity is not only a strategy to address issues of cohesion on a rumbling team, but also a spiritual practice for the Church to celebrate the gifts within us and prepare for the kin-dom among us (Mt. 4:17).

Luckily, the Church has the right coach for the job—Jesus.

It feels a bit odd to say, but Jesus and Coach Lasso have similar coaching styles. Rarely in the canon do either one of them lead in such a way that usurps communal authority. In fact, rarely do either of them give an answer without telling a story that makes you have even more questions, and that is not by accident. It is because curiosity empowers people to lead by example, divesting power from any one person into every single person. Sure, Coach Lasso will make top-down decisions like setting the lineup for a game, but when Nate has an idea for a play, Ted is curious about its design and efficacy and then asks Nate to lead with his own gifts. In the same way, Jesus will say directly, "You shall love your neighbor as yourself" (Mt. 22:39), but he also teaches others through his own curiosity how to lead for themselves. Jesus never tells the disciples how to talk about him, but rather asks, "Who do people say that the Son of Man is?" and, "Who do you say that I am?" (Mt.16:13,15) so that the disciples, the members of his team, gain the skills necessary to lead with their own gifts but also learn to be open to the gifts of others. Neither Jesus nor Coach Lasso see the success or failure of the team as their responsibility alone; rather, they understand that much like faith, success looks a whole lot more like trust than a trophy. And that is because they both know that curiosity is foundational to relationships, and relationships aren't about what is gained; they are about what is shared.

Of course, you can be curious and not be a team player. You can be curious for selfish gain—say, by appropriating traditions and cultures under the guise of curiosity. But that won't build relational trust, and the hermeneutic of curiosity is built on relationships. That is why, like any good team strategy, the hermeneutic of curiosity needs practice.

Neither Coach Lasso nor Jesus is curious about just one thing or at just one time. The hermeneutic of curiosity is a leadership model and a practice in every part of their lives. We are called to practice, not just to learn but to grow and improve. Parables aren't just stories, they are the call to practice because parables teach us that people rarely get it right the first time. So we need to mess up and keep trying. We need to be curious as to why it didn't work, who are we missing, and how we might fix it. And practice, like faith, is both personal and communal.

When you practice as an individual player, you can fine tune your own gifts and skills, and the growth will eventually come. But when you are on a team and in relationship with others, then growth becomes exponential because you don't just learn from your own successes and mistakes; you get to learn from others. Curiosity is a holy commitment to relationship, but it doesn't mean that it isn't also vulnerable and uncomfortable at times. Being curious shows your own space of interest and vision for growth, but it can also show your growing spaces; and that can be a truly humbling experience, especially in today's society that equates perfection with competency. Yet sharing the fullness of ourselves gets easier the more you do it and the more you see others share as well. Jesus and Coach Lasso know this, which is why their leadership is often shown through personal examples. They both lead with curiosity in themselves and others by sharing not only their strengths but also their growing edges.

Take Jesus and the Canaanite woman of Matthew 15:21–28. This story offers us a great insight as to how curiosity, when held tenderly in conversation with certainty, helps others to grow in their own faith for the sake of communal health. Jesus is certain in his mission, yet when curiosity enters the conversation between Jesus and the Canaanite woman, we get growth from every person. A hermeneutic of curiosity in life and faith helps everyone grow, from Jesus to us and from coach to player. Much like how the Gospels share in part the vulnerable stories of Jesus's life, *Ted Lasso* also shares some of the tender growing moments of Coach Lasso's life.

Coach Lasso's mental health is an ongoing theme in the show; he shares his experiences with panic attacks and therapy, inviting others on the team to vulnerably name their own experiences and needs. Through this learning, he becomes curious as to how a professional mental health doctor might be beneficial to the health of his staff and players as well as the overall success of his team. In Season 2, Episode 1, Coach Lasso brings on Dr. Sharon Fieldstone (albeit reluctantly, but this curious life of faith is not always easy!), and this new team member makes all the difference. Both Jesus and Coach Lasso share their stories as an invitation for curiosity in another's life, not because they are certain of their results but because they know being curious about unknown gifts, communities, and people is the best way to build your team and build the kin-dom.

There will always be places where God is at work that are unknown to us, but if we want to build the kin-dom, if we want to resurrect rather than relegate, then we need to be curious with ourselves, with each other, and maybe even especially with God. The hermeneutic of curiosity within *Ted Lasso* teaches the Church that certainty may feel comfortable, but it won't make you the best team that you can be. If Jesus is our coach, then we are Jesus's team, called to learn and grow together with a vision for communal care through genuine curiosity and authentic answers. We can show up, put on our uniforms, and even know every aspect of the game, but until we ask what position everyone plays or what injuries our players have, then we won't know the best way for the team to come together. Let's face it: it is going to be a challenge to score a goal if your whole team only plays defense. But as *Ted Lasso* shows us, if you are curious only about the ways a person can help the team win and not about the wholeness of the player, you will always do more harm than good.

When he is new to the team, as someone who believes in earning trust and not asserting authority, Coach Lasso doesn't just ask about player positions, but who the players are at their core. There is a difference between Coach Lasso talking to the players about their game play and Sam sharing with Coach Lasso about his father. In the same way, there is a difference between the questions, "Who am I?" and, "Who do you say that I am?" Both give us information about the other, but neither tells the whole story of what you and God are doing together. When you are curious, genuinely curious, you also listen. And holy listening will always lead to more questions. Holy listening paves the way forward with curiosity rather than certainty.

The Church and our local congregations are still very much in the game, though many of us fear relegation. We have called up new players, and we are helping established players see what is yet to come; but somewhere along the line, in the planning of the next game and the anticipation of the next season, we have forgotten to be curious about what is happening now. We concern ourselves with the certainties of communal life, like Sam's youth and the imminence of Roy's retirement, and we forget to be curious about what these two professional footballers might teach each other—Sam, a Black, young, Nigerian-born player and Roy, a white, older, British-born player. Our certainties about one other keep us from being curious about why the team trusts Keely so quickly. We skip the questions around Colin's loves outside of soccer, and we miss asking Coach Lasso and Dr. Sharon why they took these jobs in the first place. What we do is only a part of who we are, but there is so much more to each of us and all of us if we are curious. We have postured ourselves to think that what we do for the Church is who we are to the God, rather than the other way around. But curiosity can help us fix that error.

Our universal humanness that encompasses the unique spark of God that resides within each of us calls us all to the crucial work of our team: the Church. But not every story is ours to know just because we ask. Authentic sharing and relationships take time and trust. So continue to remain curious and receive the gift of holy stories about God and God's people. Remember that the hermeneutic of curiosity pairs best with holy listening. We all have the necessary gifts to build God's kin-dom and avoid relegation faithfully and successfully, but only if we can lead with curiosity and covenant with each other. Then we might ask the questions no one thought to ask and receive an answer from God that no one ever expected. And even when you're building the kin-dom through the hermeneutic of curiosity and your team is playing well—meaning they are present and curious to the gifts of one another—there will always be some things about God and each other that will always remain a mystery. Yet if we turn to the playbook of our Coach, we know that trust takes time. So be patient, and when the time is right and the Spirit moves, try starting by asking what God is calling you to do this season. Or, if you're really wanting to go deep, ask, "What does barbecue sauce have to do with darts, Ted?" Then wait for the bullseye.

We may never know about the depth of Coach Lasso's relationship to barbecue sauce, but we will remain curious—curious with God, with the church, and with each other—for Richmond...for the kin-dom.

Reflection Questions:

- What are the hermeneutical ethics you live by?

- Are you still curious about Jesus?

- What is something surprising about you?

- What is a spiritual gift you are great at but not passionate about?

- What part of the Church would you like to learn more about?

- What scares you about the Church?

- What is something that is not historically called "church" but feels like it?

- How do you feel about team sports?

Chapter Four

Forget What's Behind: Sanctified Imagination and *The Harder They Fall*

The Reverend Rae Karim

"Forgetting what's behind and reaching forth to what's ahead, I press toward the mark of the high calling in Christ Jesus." These are the words verbally shared and authentically captured by the apostle Paul in Philippians 3:13–14. These are the words that rang loud and clear to me as I reflected on the hit Netflix film, released October 2021, *The Harder They Fall*.[38] It was a pretty good movie, complete with a nice soundtrack and a star-studded cast that also debuted new faces. It wasn't just any old movie. It was a new-age Black western that took us along through a fictional storyline, using the names of real-life western heroes and heroines.

So how does a Black western and the words of the Apostle Paul end up in a literary collaboration? I'm glad you asked.

The crux of this movie is based on a memory of Nat Love, our hero, but it's not just any memory, like a childhood memory of sunny skies, filled with the background noise of laughter and fun. It is a gritty, violent memory, in which Nat Love's parents die right before his eyes. It is a formative memory for Nat, for the plot, and for the viewer.

Our eyes are some of the main players when it comes to our memories. Along with sounds and smells, sight adds to the capacity and character of what our minds hold onto. Still, there are times where memories are etched into our brains for several other reasons, like fear, pain, or hope. The first five minutes of this movie spare no guessing with that embedded etching, literally. Young Nat Love had a cross etched (or really more like carved) into his forehead as an everlasting memory of what his young eyes and now broken heart had witnessed.

It didn't take long before that young broken heart became a grown vengeful one. And who could blame him? After all, a strange man interrupted their family dinner, killed his parents, and left a literal mark on the center of his forehead—and a cross at that! What audacity! Perhaps some would call the mark one of faith, though that would be a stretch; neither faith nor its root, love, are meant to hurt in that way. I'd venture to say it was the mark of an unforgettable, unrelenting experience. Every time he saw himself, he saw that mark. Every time he saw that mark, he heard, saw, and remembered that evening.

It is impossible to forget, and yet the Apostle Paul (AP moving forward) encourages us in Philippians to forget what's behind. There are two questions that come to mind, AP: first, why *should* we forget some things? Second, how *can* we forget those things?

Using what one of my childhood pastors would call my "sanctified imagination," along with a few context clues and some theological study, I believe I can answer the first question. Why should we forget some things? We should forget some things so that we can reach forth to what is ahead. Put another way, that which we are remembering has the potential to hold us up and hold us back. It is like reaching for the door that leads to freedom with one hand while the other is still bound. Not all memories are worth holding on to, right? I mean, who wants to remember the first time they (fill in your own blank) because having these memories is both an individual yet universally shared human experience. So ironically, we all have memories we don't want to hold on to, but for some reason, they remain.

AP's words still ring clear...forget what's behind. So here we are with our second question: how do we forget some things— certain things, specific things, especially the things we want to forget? Is it even possible to truly forget? Was AP being literal or figurative here? I thoroughly enjoy word study, and this is the perfect time for it. And there are few words better to dive into than *forget*. My go-to for word study is *Blue Letter Bible,*[39] and it did not disappoint. The word *forget* means to no longer care for, to give over to oblivion. And who knows, maybe that is what AP was hoping for with his encouragement to us—forget what's behind so much that the memory washes away in a sea of nothingness.

But when you have a cross carved into your head by the man who killed your parents, forgetting is hard to do, AP! It just is. Still, there's a beautiful irony in that Nat Love found a way to navigate that memory. He didn't forget it because he couldn't forget it. So instead, he used it to fuel his way forward. He used it to reach for what was ahead. And for him, that meant vengeance. That meant taking out the man who took out his parents and took unwarranted rights to be a creator by etching that cross in his forehead.

Nat Love had a way to navigate his trauma, and no, it wasn't necessarily the best way, it wasn't necessarily the right way, but it was *his* way. It was his way of reframing the memory. Speaking of, could that be what AP meant, reframe what's behind? It's worth considering, especially because again, we don't want to remember some memories, and some of those same memories we don't know how to forget or give over to oblivion. Neither our brains nor our bodies know exactly how to truly forget.

So how, AP? How do we forget? How do we give those memories over to oblivion? How was Nat Love supposed to forget, given that every time he mounted a horse, every time he robbed a bank, every time he deployed his weapon, every time he caught a glimpse of himself and that forehead marking, he was reminded of his reason why: vengeance. Yes, I know there are the scriptures that speak to vengeance, particularly, "'vengeance is mine, I will repay,' says the Lord" (Rom. 12:19). I also know David asked the Lord in Psalm 13, "How long?" because sometimes it looks and feels like *God be taking too long.*

Nat Love had waited long enough. He waited his entire childhood. He waited through his teenage years. He waited well into his young adulthood. Now the time had come—not only to come face to face with the memory, but also face to face with the person who was responsible for the memory: Rufus Buck.

Buck was a known outlaw who was on his way to jail, that is, until his posse came to set him free. Once that happened, Buck wasted no time beginning his reign, rule, and takeover. It was obvious he didn't know how to forget either—and he didn't let others forget. He reminded them that he was in control, and there was nothing they could do about it.

Nat Love wasn't one of them. He knew there was something he could do about it. He knew it because he'd planned it his whole life. Nothing and no one would stop him on his journey toward vengeance that he felt was rightly his. Buck had his gang. Nat Love had his gang. All involved parties had pretty good experience with weapons and war. There would be no backing down or giving in. Though this battle was ultimately between

Nat Love and Rufus Buck, their collective comrades were in it to win it with them.

Every punch and every pop of their gun was not about forgetting—not by any means. It was about an active memory. It was about what happened, who did it to whom, and why. It was about where it took place and when. It was about how the memory was formed. That was their way of reaching forth to what was ahead. And what was ahead for them was freedom. Freedom from the other warring party, freedom from the memories, freedom from the pain. The irony is that most of those involved wanted freedom from Rufus Buck's unscrupulous ways. All who were on the side of Nat Love gave it all they had, even when it meant they gave their lives. Memories will make you do some interesting things, won't they?

> Forget. Give it over to oblivion.
> Give over to oblivion the fact that his parents were killed?
> Give over to oblivion the fact that he had a cross etched into his forehead by the killer?
> Give over to oblivion how he was haunted day in and day out by those moments?
> Not Nat Love.
> He couldn't forget.
> But he could reframe.

He couldn't reframe the memory of what was, but he could and would create a new memory of what was going to be.

Yeah! AP, maybe that's how. Maybe it's not about forgetting what's behind per se and not about reframing it either. Maybe the way to reach forth to what's ahead is to create another memory. This memory should be better than the previous one. It should be better and bigger and more memorable. Now, of course, I automatically think happier and more fun. Bring in the sunshine and the laughter, right?

However, that is not always the case. Not all new memories are fun memories. Still, they have their task: to move the former memory into oblivion, or not. When it came time for Nat Love and Rufus Buck to finally have their face-to-face match, Philippians 3:13 was nowhere to be found. One of the best scenes of this movie had everything (and I do mean everything) to do with remembering. It had everything to do with looking at, feeling, seeing, smelling, and touching everything that was behind. Oh, I don't even think Lot's wife had anything on this *look back*. Word for word, line upon line, and precept upon precept, Rufus Buck took us there. He took us on a journey down memory lane and he took his nemesis Nat Love with him.

On this journey, Nat and Rufus are alone, finally. On this journey, Nat tells Rufus, "pick up your guns." He was ready for battle. He was ready to remember that day one last time, so he could hopefully and finally forget it by taking the life of the man who changed his life forever.

But something else happened: yet another memory. This time, from the unlikely source of Rufus. Sorry, AP! That Philippians scripture just didn't stick with them after Sunday School class.

Rufus begins a conversation with Nat, asking if Nat's father was a good man. Nat responds that he and his mother were good people before Rufus killed them.

Rufus says that they, Rufus and Nat, had different upbringings. Nat wants to hear nothing of it. Nat's ready for the gun war, but Rufus continues with...a memory.

Rufus tells Nat that Rufus's father was very abusive. Rufus tells Nat one day Rufus decided to intervene because essentially, enough was enough.

It didn't fare well for Rufus because his father then took it out on him. Rufus tells Nat his father wasn't a good man; rather, he was a bank-robbing outlaw who liked to drink.

As he chooses to remember, he tells Nat his father left Rufus and his mother, taking everything with him. He tells Nat he was ten years old, just like Nat was when Rufus etched that cross into Nat's forehead. He tells Nat he searched for his father because he wanted revenge. He tells Nat that after searching for so long, he finally found him and that his father was a new man.

Not only was he a new man, but he was also a clean man with a church. Can we accept that finding God "clears the past" until it doesn't? You see, AP, there's something about forgetting what's behind that really is more challenging than we think. And again, I ask *how*? Not so much how *we* do it, but how *you* did it? Are there any tips or tricks you can share?

Nat and Rufus sure could have used those tips, especially when Rufus reveals to Nat that they have the same father. Oh, but it goes deeper than that. Not only do they have the same father, but they are of the same outlaw heritage. The one thing Rufus didn't want to become, he became—just like his father. And the hard-to-accept truth for Nat is that although Nat thought his ways had more to do with vengeance for his parents, he learned, on the journey down memory lane, that it had everything to do with his bloodline. To forget what was behind was damn near impossible because it was the reason he reached for what was ahead: the opportunity to mend the broken pieces of his heart.

So I ask AP, what do we as the church do with our memories? The institutional memories that bring comfort to some and harm to others? The personal memories that hold us close even when we seek to set them free? How do we as a Church, AP, move forward when scripture, community, and lived experiences tie us to what was and hold us back from what is, to the detriment of what could be? I don't expect you to write back, so I think we need to turn to prophets like Rufus and Nat, who call the church forward not with the wisdom of the ages, but with the truth of the now. Truth sets Nat and Rufus free, and so will truth in Christ for the beloved communities we serve, seek, and build.

Reflection Questions:

- What is the most vivid memory you have, and what senses do you associate with it?

- Is vengeance Christian?

- What is in your past that you haven't left behind, and what do you need to do in order to let it go?

- What are you pressing toward with Jesus Christ? Is it for you alone, or you and a community?

Chapter Five

Lord, Only You Can Answer That: Dry Bones and *Get Back*

The Reverend Travis Smith McKee

When you imagine a holiday gathering with family, what do you picture? A table full of food, cousins from out of state that you see every other year? Tons of down time to play cards, catch up on family gossip, or to watch a nine-hour in-depth TV documentary that people have been waiting 52 years to see? Wait...what? Somehow, over Thanksgiving of 2021, many people did just that!

The last album of The Beatles, *Let It Be*, was fully documented as it came together, with over sixty hours of video and one hundred and fifty hours of audio recorded. Famed director Peter Jackson spent years with this footage, sifting through all the dailies and clips to find the best moments and string together a story that needed to be told. In the end, it was a documentary series that was equal parts nostalgic and inspiring. It was filled with history, people, stories, and songs that were familiar; yet the overall story was entirely new. The series was called *Get*

Back, and it quickly became the perfect place for established fans to start a new journey with The Beatles and for those less familiar to be just as engaged. As a director, Jackson is known for the *Lord of The Rings* film franchise, but not necessarily for his brevity. He originally took the collection of *Get Back* footage from sixty hours down to eighteen hours, and even he knew that no one—not even the most diehard fan of the Fab Four—was going to sit in a movie theater for eighteen hours. However, the pandemic and the prevalence of streaming services gave him an alternate vision for the story and its distribution. The final cut, closer to nine hours, was broken down to three episodes and aired on Disney+.

At some point, even the most devoted fans of The Beatles might ask, "Can there really be nine hours of worthwhile material?" Well, I can attest personally that there is little difference between the seventh and nineteenth time they run through, "Don't Let Me Down." But what's fascinating about this show is that we are invited to observe a deeply personal and vulnerable artistic process. Here are four of the most famous men in the world, in a band unable to tour because any public appearance is immediately drowned out with ecstatic screaming fans. To be allowed into this process of recording is a privilege. The intimacy and humanity of the footage is a gift that invites us to be present with four friends and their community.

In the midst of strewn yet strategically placed recording equipment and buzzing producers, we see four friends getting together in a room to make music. Surrounded by friends and spouses, they let loose and goof around until these loose riffs become melodies that eventually turn into songs. There is a moment in the series where Paul McCartney, Ringo Starr, and George Harrison are sitting around the room together.[40] Paul starts absentmindedly strumming on his bass while George and Ringo are waiting for new microphones—yawning. But as Paul strums, plucks, and plays to no one in particular, they hear something in the rhythms and barely formed melody. In the span of just a few minutes, they go from relatively nothing to the outline of their next big single, "Get Back." With Paul on bass, George joins in on his guitar and Ringo starts drumming with his hands on his lap—it's a song! As people of faith, we deeply value the process of creation, and what a joy and holy moment it is to witness the creation of one of the biggest songs ever!

Get Back was released Nov. 25, 2021, Thanksgiving Day, and during that time, my dad and I talked a lot about this series. He and I will talk about most movies, music, and TV shows (so probably this book, too!), and discuss ad nauseum. Yet it is with the art from the 1970s era where he really gets to shine. Some of the *Get Back* footage originally came out in 1970, and my dad told me about the day he saw it in the theater. He had skipped school and remembered everything about seeing it that day... including the lore surrounding the timeline. By May 1970, The Beatles had officially broken up, and this album and film were released posthumously. With a dark cloud hanging over them, everyone going into that theater was looking for an answer to what went wrong...what happened here to make the biggest band in the world cease and desist?

So my dad was beyond excited to see this again, and as we talked about it, I learned about the differences he saw between the original movie, *Let It Be*, and *Get Back*. I told him I was looking forward to watching the original movie and my dad quickly quipped back, "You can't! You can't watch the old movie because it's not available anywhere." He had to be wrong; this is the age of the Internet. I can watch just about any movie at literally any time I choose! And yet, some research proved my dad right. *Let It Be* never had a wide home entertainment release. It was only released on LaserDisc, which is a challenge to procure, let alone play, in 2021. A film about the biggest band in the world was not widely distributed for four generations of media players, meaning this project was all but dead until it was...resurrected.

Enter Peter Jackson. This director wanted to work on this legendary film because he has loved The Beatles since he was a kid.[41] In 2017, Jackson approached Paul McCartney, one of the two Beatles still living (Ringo Starr is also still alive and working), about making a new version of the film. Paul was hesitant. Paul did not want to revisit the end of The Beatles— surely, he may have felt uneasy from the film's initial reception, which suggested he was to blame for the band's breakup. He was happy to let the past be the past and to let the project stay dead. That was until Peter Jackson was given access to all the footage and tuned in to what was actually on the tapes. Where Paul and the original director saw an ending, a death of the band, loss, and sadness, Peter Jackson saw new life, new meanings, and was excited to give this story a chance at renewal.

The new footage brought to life the joy a beloved band shared as they smiled, laughed, and created together. There was footage of the band's children in the studio, playing drum parts and horsing around. It showed the renewed energy that came when their friend Billy Preston walked in the room and began filling in the songs with exciting organ licks and chords on the Rhodes piano. The footage captured the connection these lifelong friends had, especially Paul and the band's legendary fourth member, John Lennon. Paul and John were constantly goofing around, making eyes at each other, and enjoying the deeply moving and connected process of making music together. Jackson said if the footage "lived up to the notorious reputation of The Beatles breaking up, and it being a horrible time for them, and they were depressing, I don't think that I would have made the film. I would have said, 'Sorry, get someone else to do it.'"[42] Needless to say, when Jackson tuned in, he found joy and a sense of renewal.

Jackson felt he needed to do one thing to make this film really come alive again: it needed color correction. He worked with an editor/colorist and adjusted the look of the film to make the picture brighter and feel more welcoming. The colors of the early 1970s started to pop again. The first scene of the movie is a literal film studio with vivid colors shining behind them and yet the original film muted these colors. The original film emphasized the rainy rooftop concert, but through reprocessing, Jackson showed the electricity of their first public performance in years. From this dead movie, released at the nadir of Beatlemania in the wake of the band's very public breakup placing a literal lens of darkness over it, a vibrant story of grace, joy, and friendship came to life. It had to be told, this time through a different vantage point. The right perspective and loving kindness gave this story the gift of presence, renewal, and possibility.

The prophet Ezekiel wrote to a people conquered and exiled. As a prophet, he was also living in his people's situation. Israel, once the promise of God's people, the shining example of God's ways in the world, was now oppressed and nearly extinguished. God's promises seemed concluded and unfulfilled—God's promise to Abraham of descendants that outnumbered the stars and the renewed covenants through Isaac and Jacob, Moses and Joshua, and David and Solomon. Were they all gone? Was the entire story of the people of God finished, after all they had been through? Was it all for nothing?

Ezekiel was a prophet who saw vivid images from God's promises, and the valley of the dry bones was no exception:

> I felt the powerful presence of the Lord, and his spirit took me and set me down in a valley where the ground was covered with bones. He led me all around the valley, and I could see that there were very many bones and that they were very dry. He said to me, "Mortal man, can these bones come back to life?" I replied, "Sovereign Lord, only you can answer that!" (Ezekiel 37:1–3 GNT)

Ezekiel could see the bones…dry and bleached from the sun as the remnants of life, as evidence of life that had been but was no more. Can bones come back to life? No! They are dead, so why even ask? Yet Ezekiel, the prophet in the presence of the Lord, wanted to believe the Lord had a reason for asking this. Still, Ezekiel didn't even want to say that he could see the bones come back to life. He didn't want to pretend that he knew what could happen, so he turned it all over to God, "…only you can answer that!"

> He said, "Prophesy to the bones. Tell these dry bones to listen to the word of the Lord. Tell them that I, the Sovereign Lord, am saying to them: I am going to put breath into you and bring you back to life. I will give you sinews and muscles and cover you with skin. I will put breath into you and bring you back to life. Then you will know that I am the Lord." (Ezekiel 37:4–6 GNT)

I had a friend who gave me a new perspective on a familiar verse: "Ask and it *will* be given to you, seek and you *will* find, knock and the door *will* be opened…" (Mt. 7:7 NIV *emphasis mine*).

So often, we skip over the *will*, as if the word of God is not speaking with certainty—I *will* give you sinews and muscles, I *will* cover you with skin, I *will* put breath into you and bring you back to life. Only the Lord can answer this, and the Lord does, definitively. Ezekiel spoke the prophecy, and as he did, he saw it come true: the sinews and muscles came back, the flesh came back, the word of God came back. It became a real and lived experience; the winds came and breathed life back.

The prophet Ezekiel sought restoration and renewal. He searched for new life, and he could not see it on his own. The promises of God were invisible to his eyes, yet God could see. Ezekiel did not settle for his own viewpoint; he trusted God's to completely show him the life coming back. This was not just some fever dream or strange vision. It was a promise to the people of Israel, a direction for the people to the promise of God, even as they sat in exile, even as billboards could have read, "ISRAEL IS OVER."

> God said to me, "Mortal man, the people of Israel are like these bones. They say that they are dried up, without any hope and with no future. So prophesy to my people Israel and tell them that I, the Sovereign Lord, am going to open their graves. I am going to take them out and bring them back to the land of Israel. When I open the graves where my people are buried and bring them out, they will know that I am the Lord. I will put my breath in them, bring them back to life, and let them live in their own land. Then they will know that I am the Lord. I have promised that I would do this—and I will. I, the Lord, have spoken." (Ezekiel 37:11–14 GNT)

There's a certainty that the prophet has. He is not seeing it from his own perspective, but from God's—the God who has been holding onto hope for them, who has kept the promises for them, and who has been the source of peace and grace. And the circumstances of the present do not and cannot negate God's promises. God *will* make restoration, healing, grace, and peace a reality for them—a reality in which dry bones gain muscles, flesh, and breath as they re-enter a living, breathing reality.

In the valley of loss, how often do we view loss as the end? When we are surrounded with despair and hope is long gone, do we forget the joy and promises we felt before? Loss is real. Pain is real. They are both unavoidable and a hard part of life, but they are not the end. Pain, loss, and disappointment do not negate the promises of God. God's promises endure. God's promises restore. God's promises name God's perspective—a perspective of creation, restoration, and hope, even if we cannot see it.

I doubt that Peter Jackson is going to come to you anytime soon with 60 hours of footage from your past (If so, how in the world does he have that?), but the perspective he brought of hopefulness, restoration, and renewal—that perspective is not his alone. Where does our hope come from? Can the dry bones ever see life? If we tune in and search for God, is there a refreshed vantage point we need? Do we get renewed? Lord, only you can answer that!

Reflection Questions:

- Who would you trust to tell the story of your life? What things would they need to know about you? What stories would you want to be sure are included?

- How have you experienced the resurrection of something you thought was dead, ended, or over?

- How do you experience confidence in God? Can you describe it?

- For your community, what moments need to have a broader or new perspective?

- What time in your life would you like to experience again? How might you share that time with people today?

- What is your favorite song and why? Where do you see God in it? How does it renew your spirit?

Chapter Six

The Sun Has Gazed on Me: Song of Songs, Beyoncé's *Black Parade*, and Decolonization

The Reverend Larry J. Morris III

How might we honor our unique cultural identities and be true to our Christian faith? This chapter focuses on Blackness and African spirituality, but the lessons can be applied to multiple identities.

> I am black and beautiful,
> O daughters of Jerusalem,
> like the tents of Kedar,
> like the curtains of Solomon.
> Do not gaze at me because I am dark,
> because the sun has gazed on me.
> My mother's sons were angry with me;
> they made me keeper of the vineyards,

but my own vineyard I have not kept!
(Song of Songs 1:5–6)

The Song of Songs (also known as the "Song of Solomon," "Canticles," and "the Song") is notably different from the other books of the Bible. Renita Weems notes two ways in which the Song is sharply contrasted against other books in the Bible:[43] the absence of the mention of God's name and the absence of allusions to Israel's religious traditions.[44] Weems does note a possible religious allusion to the Garden of Eden story: "the lovers exchange their love poems against the backdrop of a pastoral, utopian garden setting where images of animals, hillsides, and exotic flowers predominate."[45] Other than this possible allusion, there are no explicit theological claims in the Song. There are no divine judgements or pleas for divine help. The Song does not easily tie into the larger story of the people of Israel. The Song is about love. Sensual love. Romantic love. It's named the Song of Songs for a reason. There is no greater love song than this poem. It is also about self-love and love of community as we see in Song of Songs 1:5–6. Maybe that's why this book is included in our canon. The Song provides us insight into the inner workings of biblical Israel. Or at least, the inner workings of a few people in Israel—a woman and a man longing for each other and a group of women providing commentary to this sensual love affair.

In the midst of this sensual love poem, we cannot miss the acts of resistance. This is the only book of the Bible that fully showcases a woman's voice. Not just any woman but a self-identified Black woman. A Black woman who calls herself "black and beautiful." This Black and beautiful woman speaks for herself without the voice of a presumably male narrator. Weems notes:

> where more than fifty-six verses are ascribed to a female speaker (compared to the man's thirty-six), the experiences, thoughts, imagination, emotions, and words of the anonymous, black-skinned woman

are central to the book's unfolding. Moreover, the protagonist is not merely verbal; unlike many of the women in the Bible, she is assertive, uninhibited, and unabashed about her sexual desires.[46]

The anonymous Black woman is also assertive, uninhibited, and unabashed about her Black skin being beautiful. Other examples of acts of resistance in the Song include the voices of the daughters of Jerusalem and the mention of the "mother's house" (vv. 1:5; 2:7; 3:4–5, 10; 5:8, 16) whereas the "father's house" (Gen. 24:38, 47:12; Num. 30:3, 16; 1 Sam. 18:2, 22:11) is typically mentioned in other books of the Bible. After declaring that her Black skin is beautiful, she rebukes those who stare at her because her skin is dark. She mentions the injustice she faced by her mother's sons because they were angry with her. We are not sure why these men were angry with her. Could it be that she had the confidence to see herself as Black and beautiful even if others did not? Might it be that working in the sun intensified her ability to see herself as beautiful just as it darkened her skin? Maybe it's because she rebuked those who stared at her. She openly laments that because of the work forced upon her by her brothers, she has been unable to do what she really wants with her life. And still she proclaims, "I am Black and beautiful." During her longing and love for another, she does not forget who she is, even if oppression has kept her from doing all that she wants to do.

In a world that continues its practice of colonization and white supremacy, proclaiming "I am Black and beautiful" is an act of resistance, and making that claim today can be the beginning of the process of decolonization. Merriam-Webster defines decolonize as:

1. "to free (a people or area) from colonial status: to relinquish control of (a subjugated people or area)"

2. "to free from the dominating influence of a colonizing power, *especially:* to identify, challenge, and revise or

replace assumptions, ideas, values, and practices that reflect a colonizer's dominating influence and especially a Eurocentric dominating influence."[47]

Some people do not see the color Black as beautiful, particularly Black skin. For many, Black skin is deplorable. Black skin is often identified with sin, evil, immorality, and a host of other negative ideologies. Not only is Black skin often seen as deplorable, but so is Blackness and Black culture. When I use the term Black, I mean a connection to the shared history and experiences of all melanated people, in all times, and in all places. There is rich diversity in those experiences. Culture can be defined as "the characteristics and knowledge of a particular group of people, encompassing language, religion, cuisine, social habits, music and arts."[48] Black culture is the characteristic and knowledge of people who identify as Black or who have been identified as Black.

One way to decolonize our faith and spirituality is to take note of the lenses in which we engage the Bible and our faith. Do we continue to associate the color Black with death, sin, and destruction, while associating the color white with life, holiness, and purity? Do we associate Black and Blackness with beauty like the Black woman in the Song? Are the experiences and culture of Black skinned people included in our "Black and beautiful" declarations? Are we still caught up in the misnomer that Christianity is the white man's religion? Christianity does not belong to whiteness or any culture exclusively. The earliest examples of Christianity—Coptic Christianity—can be traced back to the African continent in Egypt.

Europeans practiced a Eurocentric Christianity when they enslaved Africans in the Americas, and enslaved Africans infused their African religion with this new religion on American land. There has never been a pure form of Christianity, and there never will be. Christianity is practiced throughout cultures. We understand God not only through the scriptures and the traditions passed down to us, but also through our lived experience. "I am Black and beautiful" is a theological declaration echoing the Creator's words regarding creation, "It is good!" (Gen.1:31). Through decolonization, we can reclaim the beauty of our cultures and reject the oppression from colonization. One example of this in music and religion is Beyoncé's *Black Parade.*

On June 19, 2020, the day known as Juneteenth, the holiday commemorating the emancipation of those who had been enslaved in the United States, Beyoncé released a surprise single, *Black Parade.* This was soon after the murder of George Floyd and the worldwide protests in response to his killing and the killings of other Black people by police. This drop was a huge moment for pop culture and Black culture, and the public response was enormous. *Black Parade* garnered Beyoncé multiple award nominations, including the 2020 Soul Train Music Awards, the 2021 Grammy Awards and the NAACP Image Awards. It debuted on the U.S. Billboard Hot 100 at number thirty-seven on July 4, 2020. *Black Parade* became Beyoncé's fortieth Top 40 hit on the Billboard Hot 100, matching Michael Jackson.[49] On Digital Song Sales charts, it debuted at number one with eighteen thousand units sold, becoming her ninth number one on the chart, and her first solo number one since *Single Ladies (Put a Ring on It).*[50]

The chorus might be something the anonymous Black woman in the Song would say in response to her brothers and those who gazed upon her due to her Black skin:

> Being Black, maybe that's the reason why they
> always mad,
> Yeah, they always mad, yea
> Been passed'em, I know that's the reason why they
> always mad and they always have been.

The chant, "Motherland drip on me, motherland, motherland drip on me / I can't forget my history, it's her-story" is an acknowledgment of Africa and the desire to be baptized in Africa. But unlike the Black woman in the Song, Beyoncé has kept her own vineyard. So much so, she's inviting others to come around her hive and follow her parade. This parade is not just celebrating Beyoncé, but it's celebrating Blackness and Black people. During her acceptance speech for the 2021 Grammy Award for Best R&B Performance for *Black Parade*, Beyoncé said, "As an artist, I believe it's my job and all of our jobs to reflect the times. It's been such a difficult time, so I wanted to uplift, encourage, celebrate the beautiful Black queens and kings that continue to inspire me and inspire the whole world."[51]

Beyoncé's communalism is resistance against western individualism, and *Black Parade* is a song of celebration and resistance. It celebrates Blackness and resists all things that oppress Blackness. Unlike the Black woman in the Song who rebuked those who stared at her because of her Black skin, Beyoncé wants to be seen. She rebukes the negative reactions to Blackness, such as the killing of Black people by police and the systemic theft of Black labor and resources. This is why she calls for "peace and reparations for [her] people" in the song. Blackness is beautiful and should be treated as so.

Although God is not explicitly mentioned in *Black Parade,* there are theological lessons we can take from this art, particularly if we place it in conversation with the Black woman in the Song's proclamation of being "Black *and* beautiful," as well as look through a lens of decolonization. Part of the decolonization process is reclaiming our Indigenous cultures and practices, as well as honoring all other Indigenous cultures and practices. This includes finding ways to merge our Christian beliefs with Indigenous beliefs and culture. Again, there is no pure form of Christianity. Christianity is practiced and understood within particular cultures. A colonized way of understanding Christianity is to assume that anything non-white and non-

Western is sin, evil, and demonic. Every culture has good within it. Every culture honors God in unique ways. We honor God through our different cultures, not by assimilating to another.

Black Parade is an example of a Black woman owning her Black as beautiful and decolonizing American Christianity. As in the Song, the name of God is not mentioned in *Black Parade,* but Beyoncé does name Oshun and Yemonja, two Orishas (deities, goddesses) associated with the Yoruba people of southwestern Nigeria. According to Bayyinah S. Jefffries, "Oshun is typically associated with water, purity, fertility, love, and sensuality."[52] Beyoncé compares herself to this African deity, proclaiming herself as "Oshun energy." Beyoncé compares her sister, Solange, to Yemonja, "Baby sister reppin' Yemonja." Patricia E. Canson notes, "Yemonja is celebrated as the giver of life and as the metaphysical mother of all Orisha within the Yoruba spiritual pantheon."[53]

In addition to these nods to African spirituality, Beyoncé makes mention of other aspects of African culture, including the baobab tree, Ankara Dashiki print, charging crystals in a full moon, Yoruba waist beads, Mansa Musa (the tenth emperor of the Mali empire), the Ancestors, and her continual naming of the Motherland, which is the continent of Africa. Similar to the anonymous Black woman in the Song, Beyoncé is declaring, "I am Black *and* beautiful," and she includes Black culture in her declaration of beauty. Much like the enslaved Africans in the Americas, Beyoncé fuses African religious traditions with her understanding of Christianity, although again, in this song, there is no overt mention of the name God—at least not the Western, Christianized understanding of God. She reminds listeners that Black people were not birthed as slaves, but as "kings" and "tribes" who speak with "holy tongues" and "speak the glory."

In addition to uplifting African culture, Beyoncé lifts up African American culture. She begins the song declaring, "I'm going back to the South...where my roots ain't watered down." Giving a nod to where enslaved Africans first entered America. Beyoncé declares she's going back to where her roots can be traced on American soil. Her rhetoric is full of language rooted in African American culture. Words like *ice, melanin, drip, flooded,* and *fifty 'leven* are all embedded in Black American culture. She brings the image of dancing at the barbeque and looking cute and fly in life-threatening situations:

> Stroll line to the barbeque
> Put us any damn where, we gon' make it look cute
> Pandemic fly on the runway, in my hazmat.

Black *and* beautiful. She lifts up people important to Black American culture:

> Curtis Mayfield on the speaker,
> Lil' Malcolm, Martin mixed with Mama Tina
> Need another march, lemme call Tamika
> Need reparations for my people.

Malcolm X and Martin Luther King Jr. may be known by many for their contributions to social justice and liberation, but Beyoncé also lifts up two women: her mother Tina Knowles and social justice leader and movement strategist Tamika D. Mallory. In her celebration of Blackness, Beyoncé acknowledges the work that's happened to support Black thriving while also acknowledging the work that needs to be done. Beyoncé also celebrates the natural states of Black hair:

> Fuck these laid edges,
> I'ma let it shrivel up
> Fuck this fade and waves,
> I'ma let it dread all up.

Blackness is beautiful. There are nods to spirituality and communal prayer as well:

Hold my hands, we gon' pray together
Lay down, face down in the gravel

"Need peace and reparation for my people" is an acknowledgement of justice and liberation; "I can't forget my history is her-story" is a nod to the spiritual practice of storytelling and remembering. All of this is from the perspective of a Black woman who declares, "I am Black and beautiful:" a Black woman and a team of writers who declare that Blackness is beautiful and should be seen as such. So much that it deserves a parade.

Black stories like those that make up our Bible and Black stories like Beyoncé's *Black Parade* inform who we are as people of faith and help us more faithfully tune in and find God in the stories of beloved community. To name the true roots of our faith in anything besides the rich, complex, and beautiful Blackness found in our scriptures and history may reflect someone's cultural lens, but it surely isn't God's.

Reflection Questions:

- How do you celebrate Blackness and all the beauty, history, and holiness that it encompasses?

- What elements of Black culture are absent, or have been made white, in your faith and faith tradition?

- What is a song that celebrates your culture and theological views?

- How are you decolonizing your faith?

- Can you trace how your ancestors infused their Indigenous religion with Christianity?

- What are ways you talk about God without using the name of God?

Chapter Seven

The Town Where I Currently Am: The Kin-dom and *Schitt's Creek*

The Reverend Arthur Stewart

Once, Jesus was asked by the Pharisees when the [kin-dom] of God was coming, and he answered, "The [kin-dom] of God is not coming with things that can be observed; nor will they say, 'Look, here it is!' or 'There it is!' For, in fact, the [kin-dom] of God is among you." (Luke 17:20–21)

The Rose family is not very likable when they are dumped in the small town of Schitt's Creek, bought as a gag gift by video-store mogul Johnny Rose for his son David years prior. The town is the only asset the once-rich, now bankrupted Rose family has left as the series begins; they were allowed to keep it and live there because it has no value on paper. Through the first two seasons, the Rose family had these little but meaningful bursts of growth as individuals, as a family, and in their relationships, leading to the season 2 finale, where we get the first big glimpses of what I see as the kin-dom of God.

Some call it *kingdom*, some call it *reign*, and some even veer into Jesus seminary territory as they spit out *divine commonwealth*. It's not the easiest phrase to pin down, nor should it be, because the kin-dom is hard to grasp. I like the Reverend Dr. Katie Hays' definition, that the kin-dom of God is when God gets what God wants.[54] *Schitt's Creek* exemplifies the kin-dom of God, both in us and among us, by showing the characters as they transform through taking the risks of being vulnerable and accountable to one another. The kin-dom is the world not as it is, but as what it could be.

The discomfort of the status quo rubbing against the fullness of God's kin-dom coming insists upon a communal, egalitarian solidarity rather than a hierarchy of charity. Dr. Ana Maria Isasi-Diaz, who pioneered the use of kin-dom in her seminal work *Mujerista Theology*, writes:

> At the center of the unfolding of the kin-dom is the salvific act of God. Salvation and liberation are interconnected. Salvation is gratuitously given by God; it flows from the very essence of God: love. Salvation is worked out through the love between God and each human being and among human beings. This love relationship is the goal of all life—it constitutes the fullness of humanity. Therefore, love sets in motion and sustains the ongoing act of God's salvation in which each person necessarily participates, since love requires, per se, active involvement of those who are in relationship.[55]

The kin-dom of God—the alternative ordering of the world in which we are with each other, reliant on each other, and caring for one another—is among us. And this, more than anything else, is God getting what God wants, and it is what *Schitt's Creek* is about.

In a Season 4 extra available on YouTube, series co-creator and star Daniel Levy (who plays David Rose) said about the show, "It's just a bunch of people who didn't know what love was slowly learning season after season what it means to love each other."[56] This is the work of the church, the work of the local church, and the work of those who live and thrive in the kin-dom of God. We learn, season after season, what it means to love each other.[57]

This leads us back to Schitt's Creek, and how the kin-dom came roaring in at the end of Season 2.[58] The main plot of this episode, at first watch, can seem like a sitcom trope—Johnny and Moira Rose turn down an invitation from the overbearing and crass mayor, Roland Schitt, and his wife, Jocelyn, for dinner at "the most exclusive eatery in Elmdale," ostensibly so the Roses can celebrate their anniversary as a couple without facilitating the Schitts' need to use a soon-to-expire dinner coupon. Johnny and Moira go to the restaurant alone, run into friends from their old life, Don and Bev Taylor, decide to eat together, and then the Schitts show up and join them. The old world meets the now world; established and begrudgingly budding relationships collide, and the Roses are caught in the liminal and uncomfortable space of transformation—a familiar place for us church folk today, don't you think?

At the dinner, as Bev and Don Taylor regale Johnny and Moira about what's happened in the world the Roses once inhabited, Don says, "You should have been there!" to which Johnny replies, "I wish we could have been." But we know, just as the Roses know, they cannot. We start to wonder if Johnny even believes it himself because, like it or not, the Roses have transformed in their short time in Schitt's Creek. Liminal space causes transformation, transformation is change, and change can be hard even for the ones on the other side of it. If you watch the full series of *Schitt's Creek* from the pilot episode through the second season's finale, there's not a definitive moment for any of the characters in which they are overtly redeemed. There is never a "Look, there it is!"; there is simply the erosion of what came before and the hope for what is yet to become. It is a subtle, nuanced change, perceived only to those that have lived it, until it is brought to light when the Schitts come to the restaurant; the worlds of then, now, and not yet collide.

This collision had to happen, right? These comical situations are literally how sitcoms work—misunderstanding and tension are both rich sources for comedy, which is more than cheap jokes. Comedy insists everything works out in the end, that misfortunes will be reversed, and that the audience is wise to invest in the story. The Roses and Taylors make room at the table for Roland and Jocelyn Schitt; and when they are halfheartedly invited, the Schitts join the party without merit or distinction. The Schitts come as they are to the table, unapologetically. It is surely a lesson for the Church.

I am a pastor in the Christian Church (Disciples of Christ), and we are people of the table. Christ's table, always—and on our best days, tables like those in the fanciest restaurant in Elmdale as well. The Disciples center their weekly worship on the observance of the Lord's table, but it begs the question: when there is room at the table—any and all tables—do we welcome folks, or do we invite them?

If you were to come to my house in the evening, you are welcome to stay for dinner. We will share with you what we make; we will set a place for you at the table; we will grab forks and plates, pour drinks, the whole nine yards. We want you fed in body and spirit. We may not have expected you, but we want you to stay for dinner.

If I invite you to my house for dinner, and you accept, I expect you to be there unless you tell me otherwise. I will have planned a menu, I will have bought and prepared an appropriate amount of food, I will have set the table with a spot for you, and because I'm kind of hoity-toity, there may or may not be a place card with your name in a swooping script. There may even be a pie because I love making pie for guests. You are not simply welcome—you are wanted. Accepting an invitation to the table changes the lives of host and guest alike.

When Roland and Jocelyn join the table that has more than enough room for them in The Elmdale Inn, they have been invited, not simply welcomed, and that is the foundation of the kin-dom we are called to be and build together. It is hard to tell if the Schitts are wanted, though. And at the meal, it becomes clear that the shared table is a gift for some, and completely lost on others. The olive tapenade is too salty—or just perfect, according to Jocelyn. The wine is undrinkable—or it's good because it's high content, according to Roland. The table is a gift, a boon, a chance to be together as we are—or the table is just rote, routine, an acceptable distraction from what really matters: wealth, security, power, and privilege—those things that just can't fit into the kin-dom of God.

The interpretations of what the meal is about, and for whom the table is set, is most evident in the Taylors, the rich friends that providentially arrived at The Elmdale Inn, when they mock the town of Schitt's Creek. The Taylors are the Roses before the Roses began to transform...and dare we even say blossom?[59] The Taylors can't—or won't—get the name of the town right—Schittstown or Schittsville, eventually proclaiming, "and from the looks of it, the town was living up to its name."[60] They cannot see the courage, integrity, and vulnerability of those they are with, the people who, in our metaphor, *need* the table. The heckling continues as Don asks, "What do you even call someone from Schittsville? A Schitter? A Schitthead?"[61]

Have we, the church, considered the implications of what it means to be called *Christians*? The name derives simply from the Greek word *Christianos*, meaning that we are *of* Christ. It's a burdensome word, and even more challenging, to live up to the name, we must emulate and reflect Jesus by sharing and giving away our individual certainty and personal comforts for the sake of community the way Jesus did. See the challenge?

I do not believe I will be dying for the sins of humanity, expiating the great sin debt from Adam to Zebulon. But I will stand up against empire. I will bring good news to the poor. I will proclaim release to the captives. I will proclaim the year of the Lord's favor. I will eat with sinners and tax collectors. I will bless the full humanity of sex workers. But if I have not love—this is the apostle Paul now[62]—I gain nothing (1 Cor. 13:3). So perhaps to reflect, share, and emulate Christ—to be a Christian—I have to love myself and others selflessly, without ego. I have to be loved where I am, I have to love others where they are, and I have to love God, who is faithful, constant, and sometimes tells me to stop acting like a *disgruntled pelican*.

The kin-dom of God is among us when we love one another not from the top down, not as an act of condescending charity or obligated service, but as equals who just need a good meal together. The kin-dom of God is most noticeable among us when salvation and liberation are held together in love for each of us and all of us. The kin-dom of God is salty olive tapenade and high-content fruit wine (surely from the Herb Ertlinger Winery) at a big table in Elmdale.

At dinner, when Roland is mocked, made to feel unwelcome, and minimized by the Taylors, Johnny Rose finally gets it—he finally dies to his old life, a life that had already left him for dead, and finds resurrection in the kin-dom. He tells his former friends, the Taylors,

> Here's the joke—the joke is I'm sitting here in a half-decent restaurant with my wife, and our friends, and all you two have done is complain about the food and pretend that you didn't leave us high and dry after we lost everything...I'm not quite past it. You wrote us off, Don. Not a phone call. Not an e-mail. Not a nickel. Roland and Jocelyn here could not have been more generous with what little they have. They found us a place to live. They've offered us their truck whenever we needed it.

They've invited us to their parties. They even offered to take us out to dinner tonight...And that town you passed through? It's not called Schittsville. It's called Schitt's Creek. And it's where we live.[63]

We are not privy to the rest of the conversation—why would we need to be?—but sadly, the Taylors are never seen, nor mentioned, again. The invitation to solidarity and liberation—to mutuality, as Dr. Isasi-Díaz names it—was not accepted, it seems. Which is a shame, truly. Instead, the Roses and the Schitts leave the dream deferred that was a fancy dinner in Elmdale and head back to the reality of Schitt's Creek—back to the kin-dom. When they arrive back in town, they all decide to crash the party being held at Roland and Jocelyn's son's house. Inside the party we hear music, laughter, and a community of joy. Johnny and Moira find their children, and together, they dance and share the sacred, holy, and kin-dom-affirming words of love.

In *Schitt's Creek,* the creators take every opportunity to present a world as it could be, not simply as it is. The Church would do well to follow this show's example because the kin-dom of God is not only what is and what can be, but also what *will* be. The kin-dom is ours to co-create, care for, and inhabit; the kin-dom is both *in* us and *among* us, after all. We, the church, should take note of the intentionally inclusive world created by the show, a world that shows us the best of who we are, a world that is the kin-dom of God.

The inclusive kin-dom that is *Schitt's Creek* means that everyone is accepted as they are, and this includes the characters' gender and sexuality as well. The character David Rose is unapologetically and openly pansexual—meaning he is not limited in sexual, relational, or emotional attraction based on biological sex, gender, or gender identity.[64] He is accepted in the world of *Schitt's Creek* not despite it, but simply because it is a part of him. In the previous season, David's best friend, Stevie Budd, seeks to define David's sexuality by using labels familiar to her but that are not accurate for David. Stevie's labels place limits on David—not to intentionally harm him, but so she might more easily understand. However, our identities and the language we use to identify ourselves are not up for debate to ease the growing edges and learning curves of others, especially not in the kin-dom of God—not even for our closest friends— and Stevie understands that. So, to understand, she builds an analogy around wine, saying:

> I'm a red wine drinker...and up until last night, I was under the impression that you too only drank red wine. But I guess I was wrong?

David understands, and speaks expansively:

> I do drink red wine. But I also drink white wine...And I've been known to sample the occasional rose. And a couple summers back, I tried a merlot that used to be a chardonnay...I like the wine and not the label, does that make sense?[65]

David is not told to repent or perish, he is not excluded, and he is neither chastised nor attacked in any sense of the word. He is invited into a deeper, fuller, more nuanced, and marvelous relationship with his people as who he is, and they all grow because of it.

Daniel Levy expounded more on the intentionally inclusive world he created in Schitt's Creek during a cast roundtable:

> [Creating a town fully accepting of all forms of queer identities] is the only political stand that I've taken as a showrunner...I will not show [anti-LGBTQ bigotry] at all, because I think the people learn through experiences. We're social creatures—we learn by what we watch...if you take the hate out...you're only left with joy.[66]

Like Dan, I think this world needs to see, experience, and learn from joy. Joy renews us. We need joy. We especially need joy as we build and live in the kin-dom of God anew.

We can invite the outcasts to our tables and ensure they have enough. We can reject hierarchy, dismantle power, challenge assumptions, and still have room for those with whom we disagree. We can speak honestly, value transparency, and pursue our authentic, beautiful, and fragile humanity. And we can dance, transformed by this boundless love that, season after season, renews us, restores us, and is among us when God gets what God wants.

The episode and the season end with dancing. The Roses and the Schitts crash a party attended by what seems like the whole town, meaning everyone is invited, and amidst the wider kin-dom, the Roses carve out a little place of their own on the dance floor and dance as a family. Their confessions of love to one another, their laughter, and their smiles are all signs of their resurrection and renewal, celebrating God getting everything that God wants—a kin-dom of love. The kin-dom of God is alive in Schitt's Creek, residing in the hearts, minds, spirits, actions, and relationships of its people...it's even in the wine!

And it is amongst us, too, if we just tune in to what God is doing.

Reflection Questions:

- What language do you use to talk about God's holy community?

- How do you define kin-dom?

- Does using the word *kin-dom* help you better understand God's expansive love?

- What is challenging for you about the word *kin-dom*?

- How do welcome, invitation, and kin-dom inform power and authority in your community?

- How has love changed you?

- What would it look like for your worshiping congregation to be the kin-dom of God—the world as it could be, not as it is—the way it is modeled in Schitt's Creek? What changes would need to be made? What would stay the same?

Chapter Eight

Do Our Choices Matter?
Free Will, Divine Order,
and *Foundation*

The Reverend Jason Reynolds

Once a man came to Hari Seldon and asked to be told his fate. He wanted to know whether the predictive models could chart the significance of his life. But Hari told him only the movements of masses could be predicted. The fate of one individual will always remain...a mystery. —Gaal.[67]

Of all the stories my mother used to tell me at bedtime, the Black Hole frightened me the most. It wasn't the darkness that sacred me, I was comfortable in darkness. It was the idea of an event horizon. Venture into that horizon and the gravitational pull prevents you from turning back, escape becomes impossible. —Gaal.[68]

> For those he foreknew he also predestined to be
> conformed to the image of his Son, so that he would be
> the firstborn among many brothers and sisters. And
> those he predestined, he also called; and those he called,
> he also justified; and those he justified, he also glorified.
> (Rom. 8:29–30 CSB).

I love television shows and movies that get me thinking. I'll acknowledge that some mind-numbing entertainment is needed to drown out the ever-rising levels of stress we encounter daily, but sometimes I want a great storyteller to suck me into a new world so that I may better understand the real one. The AppleTV+ series *Foundation* is one of those shows. It is based upon the award-winning novels by Isaac Asimov, one of the most influential science fiction writers of the twentieth century.

The series chronicles "a band of exiles on their monumental journey to save humanity and rebuild civilization amid the fall of the Galactic Empire."[69] One of the ideas at the center of the series is psychohistory—the sociological understanding of large masses of people, expressed in numerical form, that can be used to predict the future. Employing this idea, the series invites its viewer to go on a journey, of both space and personal exploration, to envision new lands and new ideas. Through superb character development, several thought-provoking questions are raised. What does it mean to be human? What is the essence of faith, belief, and religion? Are religion and science two sides of the same coin? What is the nature of the soul? Does humanity truly have agency, or is everything already predetermined?

Each of these ideas could warrant volumes of discussion, and many already have. But it is the last question that I am currently tuned in to. Do our actions truly matter? Do we have free will? Are our lives already predetermined? These questions hit to the core of human life. If our actions are consequential, then the significance of our actions cannot be understated. The future is yet to be written, and we each have an opportunity to grab our proverbial pen and add to the story, guided by time for future generations. Yet, if things are predetermined, do our actions ultimately matter, or is our agency a seeming farce? Without free will, is all the responsibility associated with our actions amiss?

Our beliefs related to free will or determinism have real life implications. If each individual has the ability to choose, then predicated upon those choices are innumerable possibilities. One can choose to become better, wiser, healthier, and ultimately change the trajectory of one's own life. And if one can affect their life, it would seem only logical that they could affect the lives of others—both directly and indirectly. Families, communities, nations, and ultimately humanity itself could benefit from the choices of an individual. Whether this leads to life-saving medical discoveries, transformative technologies, or just improved human conditions, free will opens a range of possibilities for improvement. And like so many others, I love a good "change your stars" story. Despite all odds and adversities, a person can still triumph. As rapper Big Sean has said, "One man can change the world."[70]

Relatedly, if free will is a reality, then one can also have a negative effect on oneself and others. Our actions and choices could devastate our future, leave relationships in disrepair, and strip away options from those around us. This seems to be the most commonly held understanding of free will. Whether it is oppressive governments, malevolent leaders, or greedy businesspersons, the idea that individual choices can have terrible consequences has proliferated through history. Highlighting the challenges that free will can provide are the discussions about COVID-19 vaccinations and what an individual's choices and responsibilities are to their communities. We cannot divorce the great responsibility that accompanies such wondrous ability.

Nevertheless, we may need to question how much agency we truly have. The aforementioned scripture, Romans 8:29–30, states that God foreknew and predestined those who would be the "elect," those who would conform to the image of God's son, Jesus. What seems to be preached from many pulpits and in most Christian sermons is the idea that we can choose God and that our choice has eternal ramifications. But what if that is not our choice at all? What if our agency and choice may be limited or not available at all when it comes to salvation?

If God has already chosen us, then none of the choices we make in our lives can affect God's choice, which predates our actions and our lives. Thus, living a good life or not would seem unconnected to one's salvation. But if this is true for salvation, might this also extend to other parts of our lives? Has God chosen the full course of our life? Is our trajectory set? Are our choices predetermined? Is free will an illusion, nothing more than us fulfilling a plan already prepared and set in motion?

This notion may be unsettling, akin to the man who asked Hari Seldon to "chart the significance of his life"[71] in search for meaning or purpose, if our choices are already predetermined. Maybe this is as frightening a circumstance as being drawn into the gravitational pull of a black hole; none of our actions or choices can change or affect the life we will lead, and we cannot improve our station or change our stars. What will be will be; we are helpless witnesses to the lives that have already been etched into time. Or are we?

In learning, concrete and defined lines and boundaries make grasping information possible and easy. But the more we learn, the more complexity is added to those boundaries. More variables can be accounted for creating far more nuance than when we originally grasped a concept. Those concrete boundaries give way to "gray areas," the blurring of boundaries. These gray areas exist sometimes because we have not spent the time and intellectual ability to gain more clarity and sometimes because the answers are still unclear. This is like learning algebra for the first time and seeing letters and numbers coexist in a math problem. This left me discombobulated, and I felt like my teacher or the "math gods" had betrayed my young mind. I now recognize the benefits, creating space to account for the yet unknown. It is not truly "gray;" it is beautiful color waiting to be filled in.

In our faith journey, we should always leave space for what we may not know, even while we hold dear what we do know. Predetermination and free will, from a theological standpoint, could be two sides to the same coin. While our learning may help us to see them in contrast, our living may help us to experience them in correlation. Thus, *Foundation* and the apostle Paul give us a bit more depth and nuance to what it truly means to be tuned into the actions of our lives and God's active participation in it. If you believe in predestination only, as Paul spoke about, what then do we do with the brokenness, hurt, and sin of the world? Does God plan our suffering, loneliness, and grief? Even more so, has God planned the great human tragedies such as genocide, the Holocaust, chattel slavery, and abject poverty? However, God's predestined plan may be easier to entertain in regard to our joys, right? I can easily imagine God meticulously planning the surprise (to you) party when you thought everyone had forgotten. I can envision the tear of sadness overtaken by deep and enduring love upon learning we had not been forgotten at all, even though it felt that way. In a life filled with overwhelming choices, predestination offers a respite—a renewal of energy and a quelling of choice anxiety for the already over-stimulated. Yet it alone doesn't quite fit our full reality or the relationship we have with God and this life.

On the other hand, free will seems to be just as prevalent a concept in scripture. Paul himself, in Romans 12:1–2, encourages listeners' active participation in the will of God, joining our actions with God's predetermined plan:

Therefore, brothers and sisters, in view of the mercies of God, I urge you to present your bodies as a living sacrifice, holy and pleasing to God; this is your true worship. Do not be conformed to this age, but be transformed by the renewing of your mind, so that you may discern what is the good, pleasing, and perfect will of God. (Rom. 12:1–2 CSB)

So, can it be both/and? This beautiful suggestion may well point us in that direction as it relates to individual choice and predetermination. I believe *Foundation* and scripture might agree on this one. On the one hand, we have visions of a life that God has laid out for us—step by step and breath by breath. A predestined life pulls us forward, whether we want to go or not. It makes us face our holy humanity in ways that feel well beyond our control, and that is because they are. And, we have the commands and strong encouragement to align our actions because they matter. They matter to us, to others, and to God. In fact, maybe the greatest image of this is Jesus himself. As he prepares for his Passion, the sacrificial giving of his life in place of humanity to provide a pathway to eternal life, he utters these words in the Garden of Gethsemane, "My Father, if it is possible, let this cup pass from me. Yet not as I will, but as you will" (Mt. 26:39b CBS). Here even Jesus, who is God in the flesh, recognizes the predetermined plan and pushes to align his own free will to it. It is both/and, as I see.

Regardless of your answer, or even God's answer, people will debate the end until the end. When the truth of the end comes—in a mystery or an event horizon—there is nothing we can do to change it. The debate regarding free will and predetermination has waged for centuries and probably will continue for centuries more. Free will advocates like Erasmus and Augustine have varied in the depth of how much freedom truly exists in our lives. Reformers Calvin and Luther, proponents of predetermination, vary in how much is already set in stone and unable to be changed. All that said, I imagine neither of these positions, in themselves, fully represent the truth. But some blend of both may be the best representation of reality—something a bit more like the blended human holiness of Jesus. So, what do you believe?

There are as many answers to this question as stars in the sky; however, whether your choices ultimately matter or not, you have an opportunity for discovery, a chance to tune into the stories of God in this world and decide what matters most to you.

Reflection Questions:

- Do you believe we have free will, are predestined, or maybe something else?

- Do your thoughts on free will/predetermination align with those of your faith community?

- Is the discussion of free will/predetermination happening in your community? What about in unintentional ways?

- Do you think of God as an active participant in your life's journey? What does that look like?

- What role does prayer play in your understanding of free will versus predestination?

- How does your life's end affect your life's journey?

Chapter Nine

One Body, Many Members: Open Minds and *Queer Eye*

The Reverend Diane Faires Beadle

Each one of us has talents and interests that set us apart from others. These gifts are uniquely ours to give, and if we don't develop and share them, the world will miss out on valuable resources that could make a difference in our neighbors' lives.

In the Netflix series, *Queer Eye*, five experts in self-improvement, the "Fab Five," use their talents to make the world more "gorge" (short for gorgeous—as hair expert Jonathan Van Ness would say). In each episode, the quintet has a week to do a full makeover on an ordinary person who needs a confidence boost. The stars of this series have built successful careers in their particular expertise: Jonathan specializes in hair styling and grooming; Tan France's focus is fashion; Bobby Berk concentrates on interior design; Antoni Porowski addresses meal preparation; and Karamo Brown helps process social and emotional baggage.

The result is more than a sum of these parts. On the surface, the person being made over gets a new hairstyle, wardrobe, and furniture. The real transformation, however, takes place in the hearts and minds of everyone involved, including the Fab Five. As queer persons, they have experienced discrimination and rejection. They know what it's like to struggle with self-acceptance. They understand that the gift of confidence they offer people is much more than one's appearance. They know better than anyone that superficial attributes like clothes, home decor, wealth, or popularity do not make a person great.

Celebrities and style gurus could easily take a condescending approach to people whose wardrobe consists entirely of camouflage or who can't remember the last time they had a haircut. Expertise all too often becomes an excuse to look down on others who don't possess our talents or advantages. The apostle Paul knew that we are creatures of comparison, trying to prove we are somehow better than the next person to secure our own sense of belonging. Paul writes:

> Indeed, the body does not consist of one member but of many. If the foot would say, "Because I am not a hand, I do not belong to the body," that would not make it any less a part of the body. And if the ear would say, "Because I am not an eye, I do not belong to the body," that would not make it any less a part of the body. If the whole body were an eye, where would the hearing be? If the whole body were hearing, where would the sense of smell be? But as it is, God arranged the members in the body, each one of them, as he chose. If all were a single member, where would the body be? As it is, there are many members, yet one body. The eye cannot say to the hand, "I have no need of you," nor again the head to the feet, "I have no need of you." On the contrary, the members of the body that seem to be weaker are indispensable, and those members of the body that we think less honorable we clothe with greater honor, and our less respectable

members are treated with greater respect, whereas our more respectable members do not need this. But God has so arranged the body, giving the greater honor to the inferior member, that there may be no dissension within the body, but the members may have the same care for one another. If one member suffers, all suffer together with it; if one member is honored, all rejoice together with it. (1 Corinthians 12:14–26)

To create a truly healthy, strong community, Paul knew that a person should use their talents or resources to care for and build up others, rather than to dominate or control. Many of us who consider ourselves Christian today would agree with the values laid out in 1 Corinthians 12. Within the church, especially, we teach that we should care for one another, no matter our position or privilege. For Paul's original audience, this would have been a much more countercultural view of relationship dynamics. Much like modern middle school, in ancient Rome, everyone had a clear place in the social hierarchy. Those at the top were expected to demonstrate their dominance over others, while those below them were expected to be submissive.[72]

Meals were one way status was on full display. In 1 Corinthians 11, Paul chastises the Corinthian church because some members eat all the food and get drunk before the others arrive to share in the communion feast (1 Cor. 11:20–34). At a typical Roman dinner party, the more prestigious guests would be seated in places of honor and served better food. No one would be expected to wait for less important guests to be served. Neither would anyone be expected to be concerned whether there was enough food for all. Paul must teach the early Christians that they are called to a different kind of community.

Social dominance was also expressed in Roman society through coercive sexual acts, in which a man of status put a subservient person in a submissive position. For Paul, the only examples of same-sex intercourse he knew of were not consensual, committed, mutual relationships between equals, but a means of exercising power over another person. It's this self-serving coercion, which humiliates and demeans those considered less important, that Paul speaks out against in many of the passages used by Christians today to condemn same-sex relationships.[73]

Paul was not concerned with the gender of one's sexual partner as much as with how one treats other people, especially other followers of Jesus. Paul had no concept of sexual orientation as part one one's innate identity. Paul had no concept of marriage based on love, same-gender or otherwise, as most marriages in his time were arranged by one's family and based on status and wealth. In fact, Paul wasn't really concerned with marriage at all. He thought Jesus' return was imminent, and therefore, there was no need to make a long-term arrangement like marriage. He was much more concerned with how following Jesus changed one's life, and he encouraged his communities to choose a way of life guided by Christian unity and care for those who had been left out. He wanted followers to orient their lives and values to a higher standard, not focused on power or personal gain but on spiritual commitment and honoring God.

As an ambassador of the gospel and as an apostle of the church, Paul advocated for changing how we think about status and how we exercise power to create a more loving community. He argued against showing one's social superiority through domination or exploitation of those who are more vulnerable. Instead he urged Christians to demonstrate their Christ-like status through genuine, self-giving love for God and for one another. To build up the body of believers, Paul taught that we should use our specialized talents and abilities to help one another thrive, so that the whole church could grow and honor God.

Some of Paul's words have been used to condemn queer people and exclude them from the church. At the heart of Paul's teachings, though, is a passion for inclusivity and acceptance, which values the diverse gifts each person contributes to the whole. When the church excludes queer persons, we miss out on the precious gifts they have to offer, gifts that bring greater healing and wholeness to the entire body. Only when we recognize that every person has inherent worth, equitable value, and inherently deserved dignity can we truly be a strong and thriving beloved community.

In every episode of *Queer Eye*, the Fab Five work together to help someone they've just met become the most authentic version of themselves. They aren't competing to create the most impressive physical transformation. It is not *that* kind of reality show, in which there are winners and losers. Instead, the Fab Five share notes they've gathered from deep, insightful conversations with that week's "hero," so they can address the person's insecurities and goals in a way that honors them. Their makeover tactics never try to change a person into someone unrecognizable. Instead, they help the person's best features shine. Often, the makeover subjects serve their family or community in meaningful ways, and they take little time for self-care. A large part of their transformation involves believing that they can have an even bigger influence on others when they feel their best.

Before Jonathan gives someone a haircut or Tan takes someone shopping for new clothes, they spend time getting to know their personality and passions, so that any cosmetic changes emphasize who they really are. These makeover artists don't impose their own style on someone else. They're not seeking conformity. Their goal is to free the person from whatever constraints have prevented them from most fully being themselves. There is a wide range of diversity in the types of people they make over. In Season 5 alone, they help a middle-aged divorced dad, a gay priest, a young Black entrepreneur, a formerly unhoused writer, a teenage environmental activist, a mom preparing for an empty nest, a bachelor deejay, a Mexican immigrant fishmonger, a pediatrician and mother of a toddler, and a fitness instructor. This list is long, diverse, and could also be known as the body of Christ.

In the first episode of Season 5, we meet Pastor Noah, a gay Lutheran priest who is still coming to terms with his own sexuality. Although he leads a congregation that openly welcomes LGBTQ+ people, he carries the shame of growing up in a church that taught him being gay was sinful. Even after coming out, he holds onto regret that he waited so long and has not spoken out more on behalf of other queer people in the church. He tells the Fab Five he has impostor's syndrome and questions whether he can really lead his church well. Noah lives in a parsonage that is so run down there are holes in the walls and mold on the ceiling. It is clear he doesn't believe that he deserves better or that he has meaningful gifts to offer the church.[74]

During their week together, Karamo arranges for Noah to meet with other queer church leaders, who share their own similar struggles and experience. He begins to realize the valuable gifts he has to offer, which the church desperately needs. As the Fab Five invest time and attention in him and his church building, Noah's energy is renewed by the visible changes. A change takes place in his spirit, too. By the end of the week, Noah tells them, "I'm becoming the pastor I've always wanted to be."[75]

It speaks volumes to have others invest in you and your work, especially because investment requires sacrifice and generosity. Interior design specialist Bobby also grew up in a conservative church that rejected him when he came out as gay. His experience was so hurtful that he never wanted to set foot in a church again. When he finds out that the Fab Five are going to a church to help a priest that week, he jokes that he's glad he's wearing his fireproof suit (a fabulous, sparkling silver tracksuit). In the process of getting to know Noah and his congregation, Bobby sees that there's hope for a new generation of young queer people who can experience love and acceptance within the church. There's a moving conversation between Bobby and Noah as the pastor apologizes on behalf of the church for the pain it caused Bobby; the wall Bobby has built between himself and Christianity begins to crumble just a little.

The apostle Paul's primary concerns for the church are that it finds unity among its diverse members and that God's love and salvation are extended to more people, beyond those who already know it. I believe Paul would applaud the ways the Fab Five use their unique talents to build up the body of Christ. They could easily use their skills and fame to make themselves seem better than their makeover subjects and spend episodes condescending to those with less impressive style and knowledge. But they never act arrogant or make anyone feel bad about themselves. They stay open to learning from the people who appear on the show and work to remove any obstacles they face that may keep them from fully using their own unique talents and well. The Fab Five use their status to help others find belonging and community, and in the process, they are transformed too.

Just imagine if each of us used our own unique talents to give the church a much-needed make-over. I'm talking about a Queer Eye-style transformation, which goes beyond superficial changes to allow the authentic, abundant hospitality of the gospel to shine its brightest. Consider what role you can play in freeing the church to be a more inclusive, genuine community that embodies Christ's call to bring good news to the oppressed and outcast. Together, we can clear away the fears and insecurities that keep us from fully embracing the beauty inherent in all of God's people. If the church is to truly flourish, we have to believe everyone's presence matters—from the very young to the well-established and everyone in between. We must treat each other as equally fabulous and necessary parts of the whole.

Let us be the kind of body that cares for everyone to whom we are connected, not looking for ways that we are superior to others, not treating others as less worthy of God's love and mercy, but rejoicing that God welcomes and cares for us all.

Reflection Questions:

- Have you ever felt less than other people? What made you feel that way? To heal, did you have to change or did others?

- If someone offered you a makeover, what areas of your life would you want to improve upon and why?

- If you could give your church a meaningful makeover that went beyond the building, what improvements would you want to make? Why? What is holding your church back from making that transformation now?

- Is there anyone who would not feel welcome in your church (or community)? Why? What is one change, for which you have the time, talent, or energy to advocate, which would make your church (or community) more welcoming and inclusive?

Chapter Ten

Where is Fat Jesus?
Sympathizing in Weakness and
My 600-lb Life.

The Reverend Dr. Delesslyn A. Kennebrew

In this age of liposuction, diet pills, waist trainers, body sculpting, gastric bypasses, bootcamps, protein shakes, Keto, Paleo, low carbs, 1200 calories, intermittent fasting, Fitbits, Fit On, BowFlex, Peloton, NutriSystem, Weight Watchers, and Noom, I believe it is accurate to say that there is no shortage of weight loss strategies. Whether one is trying to lose weight or maintain it for their own health and wellness or to become more aesthetically appealing to a certain demographic of people (perhaps even oneself?), there is a way to get to where you want to be in inches and on the scale. It will cost you time and money to eat right, exercise, or get the work done. It will require discipline and a certain level of motivation to finish whatever process one chooses to reach their physical goals. It will be the beginning or the continuation of an endless roller coaster of facing one's emotional and psychological barriers and blocks to weight loss progress. This process is not for the faint of heart. It is a billion-dollar industry, and the obsession with appearance is not going away.

So it is no surprise that there exist television shows such as *The Biggest Loser, Family by the Ton, Fit to Fat to Fit, 1000-lb Sisters*, and *My 600-lb Life*. We really are obsessed with how we look, and part of how we look involves how much we weigh. We secretly do not want to be the people who are the subject of these types of reality shows. We do not want to be described as fat, immobile, lazy, thick, plus size, large, larger, obese, morbidly obese, or any other insult directed at people who are overweight. We do not want to be *them*. Yet, we are being challenged, entertained, and yes, even inspired by their struggle.

Given our overwhelming attention to the issue of weight, it makes me wonder if Jesus ever had a weight problem. Every Jesus I have seen in pictures and sculptures is quite fit. I recognize that Jesus did not grow up in a SupersizeIt culture, but he certainly had the power to create it miraculously. He was known for blessing meals that resulted in tons of leftovers, but I do not know if that was because he miscalculated the numbers for the five thousand (not counting women and children) or if he was just really hungry—greedy, famished, starving that day—so he provided way too much food.

Now, I have read and learned that Jesus was tempted at all points, so that must also include food:

> Also, let's hold on to the confession since we have a great high priest who passed through the heavens, who is Jesus, God's Son; because we don't have a high priest who can't sympathize with our weaknesses but instead one who was tempted in every way that we are, except without sin. (Hebrews 4:14–15 CEB)

If that is the case, where is fat Jesus?

I am wondering about the Jesus who struggled with bread yet broke it and blessed it at a meal for his disciples to share from that point on in remembrance of him. Where is he in the midst of this very human struggle to disrupt the gluttonous tendencies we all have? Where is he in the midst of this very human struggle that leads to any person weighing 600 pounds? Where is he in the midst of this very human struggle to descend from such seemingly weighty heights? How is it possible for the invitation to eat bread with him at the Table to become so complicated?

The purpose of this reflection is to briefly consider the comfortability of and complications with food, and Jesus's invitation to eat, in light of reality shows such as *My 600-lb Life*. After all, Jesus' body is represented by bread, the very food item that most overweight subjects on this show are instructed to avoid for their own weight loss progress. This essay is not a condemnation of any body size or meant to affirm or cast assumptions about the relationship between weight and health. What you do or don't do with your body is between you and God, and your health is between you and your doctor. No matter what is socially said or even understood, the truth is, *everybody* and every *body* is made in the image of God, called good by their Creator, and should be valued as such in beloved community.

My 600-lb Life is described by its promoters as:

> Telling powerful stories in hourlong episodes, The Learning Channel (TLC) follows medical journeys of morbidly obese people as they attempt to save their own lives. The featured individuals—each weighing more than 600 pounds—confront lifelong emotional and physical struggles as they make the courageous decision to undergo high-risk gastric bypass surgery. In addition to drastically changing their appearances, they hope to reclaim their independence, mend relationships with friends and family, and renew their feelings of self-worth.[76]

During each one-hour episode, viewers are given an intimate picture of a year in the life of the featured individual. The episode usually begins by introducing the person who is at least 600 lbs. We are taken into their home. We see their kitchens, their bedrooms, and their bathrooms. We see their favorite chair or couch. We see their friends and family members who are presently enabling them. We see the rolls on their bodies and the limitations of their every move. We see how their homes have become prisons because they can barely move within the walls, much less attempt to leave. Some can barely walk. Most struggle with bathing. All have eating habits that are out of control.

At some point before their lives are exposed to us, they have decided to do something different. So after the introduction, we are informed that they have reached out to Dr. Nowzaradan ("Dr. Now"), the surgeon who will perform their gastric bypass surgery if certain commitments are kept by the primary subject.

The person then visits Dr. Now in Houston, Texas, and he tells them how much weight they need to lose in advance of the surgery. Understandably, he wants to ensure that they are committed to their own health and well-being because he has often explained that the surgery is not a quick fix. Every person must do the work physically and emotionally to see long-term success.

The show goes on for about an hour, and we hear about and see the struggles, tears, fights, humanness, desperation, hopelessness, and sacrifices of the person seeking to have their life transformed. Some lose the weight on target with Dr. Now's deadlines, and many do not. We see the roller coaster of emotions, excuses, and explanations around why they have or have not been successful in advance of Dr. Now setting a date for the surgery and the person relocating to Houston to continue their journey.

The diet that Dr. Now prescribes for his patients is a daily total of twelve hundred calories. This is a tremendous challenge for most of the people because twelve hundred calories is typical for one meal. They must give up a lot of foods they are accustomed to and incorporate more healthy options. One of the main foods Dr. Now suggests that they give up to experience weight loss is bread: slices, rolls, biscuits, Texas toast, bagels, pretzels, and breadsticks. Bread, a common staple in most diets. Bread, the food with which Jesus identified his body at the Last Supper:

> While they were eating, Jesus took bread, blessed it, broke it, and gave it to the disciples and said, "Take and eat. This is my body." (Mt. 26:26 CEB)

Jesus says this *bread* is *my body*. Every Sunday, once a month or quarterly in churches all over the world, we honor his command to remember him with *bread*. And every Sunday or at least once a month in churches all over the world, people who struggle with their weight just as those on *My 600-lb Life* are invited to eat that which many believe contributes to their obesity. They are invited to eat bread in some form that is not approved for consumption on their twelve-hundred-calorie food budgets. They are invited to make an exception for Jesus.

There are at least three lessons that I would like to highlight as I reflect upon this show, these six-hundred-pound individuals, and the Jesus whose body is represented by bread, the food item they must deny.

First, we all have a certain level of comfortability with dysfunction. This show is popular because we seem to enjoy being entertained by social and emotional dysfunction. On one level, we might say that it is not a laughing matter or a public matter, but plenty of people still choose to watch *My 600-lb Life* and other shows like it. We see how this weight that our bodies were not designed to carry morphs the figures of fellow humans in ways that look physically and emotionally painful and often embarrassing. However, this show and others like it continue to get the ratings needed to stay on the air; we all have a certain level of comfortability with dysfunction. We can see the dysfunction throughout the entire episode and feel all kinds of ways about it, from disgust to compassion. We watch, but I doubt if any of us pray.

Perhaps the lack of Jesus images akin to the images of the bodies we see on *My 600-lb Life* are because we have an ideal image of Jesus' size that we refuse to expand. We want to keep Jesus at a palatable size visually, regardless of if we have accounted for the accuracy of his geographical physical traits. We are not comfortable with a Jesus who is not a "normal" weight— whatever that might mean. We are not comfortable with seeing a Jesus that might remind us of ourselves or those in the show. That would be wrong to some or at least questionable to others. Our avoidance of issues such as obesity reinforces our lack of concern for the health and well-being of our neighbors.

Second, we all have experienced complications with invitations to eat and the exceptions we make to appease our peers and our appetites. The invitation by Jesus to remember and eat the bread that represents his body is complicated. We can easily say this bread does not count on our diet. We can easily say this bread is not enough to make a difference on our diet. We can easily say this bread, taken once a week, month, or quarter on our diet, will not get us off track. We can say these things and dismiss our concerns because of the portion size, but what does it really mean for those in our congregations to make an exception in the moment? Making exceptions and excuses is partially how some people got to be six hundred pounds. It is probably hard enough for these people to show up at the table, let alone worry about the criticism that might occur if they were to ask not to be served bread, the primary food, the only food, at the Communion Table. What a difficult position for people who are trying to be intentional about their own physical transformation. There is tension between accepting Jesus' invitation to eat the bread that represents his body and the commitment to reject the bread that is potentially harming the congregant's physical body, or at least delaying the realization of their weight loss goals. All it takes is one exception one time to make it easier to make an exception the next time. The communion table can be a complicated place.

Third, we all must celebrate victories great and small. While bread might complicate the physical issues faced by the participants on *My 600-lb Life*, their spiritual life can be renewed by the One who invites us to eat of the bread that represents his body. The victory embodied in Jesus' witness before and after his death, burial, and resurrection can be a source of hope for men, women, and everyone whose bodies might be a source of ridicule and discomfort.

Often, the participants on *My 600-lb Life* do not meet the initial weight loss goals set by Dr. Now. Even though they might not meet the goals, they want credit for the pounds they did lose. Every pound counts to them. So whatever they lose in the first three months—twenty pounds, fifty pounds, or eighty pounds—consistently, those who lost the weight want the lost pounds to count. They want Dr. Now to celebrate the progress, no matter how minor this victory might be to him. This comes as no surprise! We all want a pat on the back, a word of affirmation, or some kind of acknowledgement that we are making progress, getting closer to our goals, and heading in the right direction.

Every day that these participants rise and commit to their physical transformation is a day of victory. Every day that they choose to work through or work around their decision to eat bread, during communion or any other time, can bring a feeling of victory no matter what they decide. And every day is a victory for us all when we acknowledge the struggles of those who are overweight or obese with compassion and create space for them to feel supported in their health and wellness goals.

So, while we may never see an overweight, obese, or morbidly obese image of Jesus, he is ever present with all his complications to love us, support us, and sustain us as our Bread of Life.

Reflection Questions:

- What do you love about your body?

- Is there a part of you that you don't often see reflected in images of Jesus?

- What part of your faith life is most challenging for you?

- What keeps you from asking for what you need to participate fully in church?

- Is there something in your corporate faith life, such as something in worship, that you would not give up to make someone feel more accepted?

- The church has a deep history of body shaming. How might our churches start to address this? Who should lead these conversations?

Chapter Eleven

Go to Hell, Christian!
The Afterlife, This Life,
and Netflix's *Lucifer*

The Reverend Shane Isner

I must admit, I don't know what the afterlife is like or what it entails. However, with that said, when I die, I'm probably going to hell. At least, that's my hope, because then, I could meet Jesus. Lucifer, too—the chiseled-chin, fallen cherubim, who rules hell with stubbled cheeks and endearing narcissism. I mean, I would meet him (were he not a fictional character) because, after all, according to the Netflix series *Lucifer*, the devil of a man still spends most of his time in hell—by choice! Of course, doesn't everybody in hell spend time there by choice?

Before we go further, let me be candid. I have no strong beliefs about the existence of hell. Indeed, like many progressive Christians, I am both skeptical and hostile to popular notions about hell. As a youth, I attended evangelical churches who used hell to coerce teens into feeling weird about sex or adults into upping their tithes. Back then, hell scared the hell out of me! Despite my fear, I kept watching, listening, and doing what my pastors told me until I realized how ugly and harmful their strategy for community engagement and faith development was. I became curious about the truth of their misguided teachings. I had thoughts like, "Hold on, *every* non-Christian is burning for eternity?!" and, "Despite creating my hormones, God said I can't even *think* about premarital kissing?!"

What the faith leaders of those churches were teaching seemed utterly unloving despite scripture being clear: "God is love" (1 John 4:8). So eventually, I stopped worrying about outcomes and focused on my faith journey and relationship with God. I said, "To hell with hell!" I stopped thinking too much about heaven as well, since the Bible, the Good Book, ends by proclaiming, "the home of God is among mortals" (Rev. 21:3). Heaven, God's home, the place where Christians have been taught through fear or faith to hope to go, *is here* because this is where *we* are. Plus, helping "God's kingdom come...on earth" is literally in the prayer Jesus provided (Mt. 6:9–15). So my compromise has become, unless it is a funeral, I do not speculate about the afterlife. We are still in the *life* part of the afterlife. What is the point of guessing?

As *life* went on and my faith developed, I was exposed to broader and more nuanced theological depth about the afterlife, and one preacher offered me insight that has stuck with me through the years. She told a parable that originated with medieval monks. They pictured heaven as a divine city, bejeweled and sparkling, waiting to usher God's children into eternal bliss in community. Like a good city of the Middle Ages, the walls were high and gates were sturdy, but shockingly, heaven's gates were always open.

Outside the city lay individual souls curled in upon themselves, tense and anguished. Imagine them twisted into infantile positions, navel-gazing with horrified expressions, alone. They were the people who, having died, arrived in the afterlife focused entirely on themselves, *their* needs, *their* flaws or unfulfilled desires, and *their* shames, guilts, or foolish revenge fantasies. Heads slumped and shoulders bowed, they embodied for eternity the posture of sin. Individually, they were the damned.

This was the parable's hell: individuals always looking in on themselves. However, the real tragedy was not living eternally in that hellish posture. The tragedy of this hell was that if these souls just looked up, they'd see heaven beckoning with gates wide open. God's welcoming and forever love is available for anyone willing to accept it. For, as we have learned in this life, dear reader, "God is love," but that is not the end. In fact, we need to stop looking for the end in life because with God, "love never ends" (1 Cor. 13:8). However, the preacher did not end there because the point of this parable was not about the existence of an afterlife made by God, but the afterlife that we as people build ourselves. Or, as the monks put it: hell exists because we let it.

Enter *Lucifer*, the Fox-turned-Netflix show, which offers a different portrait of the afterlife with one caveat: the price for perdition is much the same as its exit. Here's a basic outline for those unaware of the show's premise: Lucifer Morningstar, the titular main character, is a devil of a man and also the *actual* devil. One day in hell, Lucifer feels the call to something else instead of torturing souls, so he relocates to Los Angeles and opens a nightclub. His new vocation renews this fallen angel's spirit through lust, booze, and notoriety. The devil feels at home in the City of Angels, but even the devil needs a hobby. Enter the LAPD, toward whose homicide investigator, Detective Chloe Decker, Lucifer is unquestionably drawn. Through his divine power of coercion (humans cannot lie when Lucifer asks them what it is they most desire), he ends up as her consultant, and together they solve murders. Their banter and romance propel the series forward until eventually Lucifer's angel status is renewed because God Almighty ("Dad") wants to retire, and who else but his favorite son should take over the family business. It's quite hilarious and spiritually insightful as well.

Season 3, Episode 7 ("Off the Record") especially piqued my interest as a pastor. As I watched, I recalled the medieval monks' parable, pondering whether I've changed my mind about hell; it turns out, I have. Not only did I change my mind about hell, but I also now desire to go there when I die...and if I'm brave enough, before I die too. To make it even better, my wife agrees, and hopefully, you will too.

The episode "Off the Record" addresses questions many viewers, including myself, have been asking such as, "Why does anyone go to hell?" and, "What's it like, anyway?" The episode opens in a hospital room with an unknown person waking up from a near-death experience. We learn that he is Reese, a Pulitzer Prize-winning investigative journalist and the estranged husband of Lucifer's therapist and one-time amorous companion, Dr. Linda Martin. Reese wants Linda back. (Please do not take lessons on healthy boundaries from the devil!) Unfortunately, through a series of events, Reese discovers Linda is sleeping with Lucifer, which drives him bonkers. So, using his investigative and reporting skills, Reese decides to expose and destroy Lucifer. Throughout the episode, hijinks ensue, a murder occurs, and Detective Decker and Lucifer rush to solve the case, in which Reese reveals himself to be less a jilted lover than a manipulative control freak. Reese, in an unwell cycle of longing for Linda, forces her to beg, "Stop saying I'm your wife. It's over."[77] A plea that has little, if any, impact on Reese.

Reese can't let go of his desire for reconnection with his estranged wife. He's trapped in an obsession to possess her and a compulsion to use her to meet his emotional needs. Reese professes love for Linda, but it is abundantly clear that this is not love. It's an abusive perversion, and Linda won't have it. To make matters worse, Reese, still hellbent on winning back Linda's affection, learns that his adversary is the genuine prince of darkness and works to find a way by which Morningstar might be destroyed. Reese remains confidently misguided and believes that bringing about the devil's downfall will win back Linda. Unfortunately, Reese's scheme goes wrong, leading to the death of an innocent woman and forcing Reese to confront Lucifer. Predictably, Reese blames the devil, and he avoids accountability for his own actions. An exasperated Lucifer responds:

> What is it with you humans, always blaming me?
> I never make any of you do anything.[78]

It is a poignant reminder of our own personal relationship to social accountability. Lucifer goes on to tell Reese a secret that he has never told a human before now:

> I take no part in who goes to hell.
> You humans send yourselves,
> driven down by your own guilt,
> forcing yourselves to relive your sins over and over.[79]

In the world of *Lucifer*, that is how hell works. We go there when we cannot forgive ourselves or others and when we fail to live compassionately or mercifully in community. And we stay in hell, reliving the shame and guilt of our lives on loop—a hell-loop, as it's called. In *Lucifer*, and as I believe in life, hell isn't God punishing humans for not following some preacher's rules. No, our own egos, shame, and unresolved pains are what lead us down perdition's path.

Lucifer continues:

> And the best part [is], the doors aren't locked. You
> could leave anytime. It says something that no one
> ever does, doesn't it?

Yes, Lucifer, it surely does say something. From medieval monks to our modern Morningstar, in this life, I have come to understand two things about the afterlife: The gates of heaven are always open, and hell exists because we let it.

I teach a Sunday school class that explores scripture and society using a progressive Christian lens. To us, that means we don't read the Bible literally, but we do take it seriously. In our study together, we value science, truth, and history. When we gather, we honor diverse religious traditions and lived experiences, and we almost never talk about the afterlife. So when I asked the class recently, "What do y'all think about hell?" they answered, "We usually don't!" If they did, they pondered all the ways humans create hell on this side of paradise. Faithful people, they figure, should worry about improving this world in this life, since too many heaven-obsessed religious traditionalists treat their neighbors demonically because of their understanding of the afterlife.

For example, a woman in my congregation (Tonya) embraced me enthusiastically when I moved to Montgomery, Alabama, from Minneapolis, Minnesota. You see, she loved Prince, like all people with good taste should. Alas, within a couple weeks of my move, the artist died. We mourned together as she shared that his music was the soundtrack for her younger life, helping her as she came out to her traditional southern family. Prince taught Tonya she could be herself and that she'd be okay.

The comfort Prince brought to Tonya worked for a while, until it didn't. Her drug addiction came and went as her family's religious disapproval only increased in virility and vitriol. I don't know why entirely, but one Saturday night three months after we had met, her wife called me and said, "Pastor, Tonya's done shot herself. At her mother's graveside."

And once again, I was called to mourn with my people as we raged at the demons she had battled for decades. Tonya had praised God with me just days previously, without letting even her wife know the hell she'd been experiencing. Some of her text messages later revealed that her family had unleashed a fresh round of religious-themed, anti-LGBTQ abuse that week, placing her right back in a hell-loop.

Several members of her family dared attend her funeral. One even pulled me aside, guilt in his pleading eyes, as he tried to convince me her pain and suffering were not his fault. "Surely, Tonya knew I only hated her sin, not her, right?" I bit my tongue to keep from screaming, "Hypocrite!" in the moment. However, later from the pulpit, I said what needed to be shared. I preached the truth: the real sin is when Christians tell gay people that God condemns them. I continued with the gospel message that we are all beloved children of the Divine. And I concluded with the message I hope they heard most—bigoted theology kills people, and Tonya is the proof.

You may not reside in the Bible Belt's buckle like I do, but I've lived enough places to know we're not as different as we think we are. All humans are "fearfully and wonderfully made" (Ps. 139:14). The fearful stains of racism pervade even seemingly well-meaning progressive communities. Poor people remain tacitly rejected from numerous churches that are more worried about carpets than hunger. And in not so many decades, we'll feel like the fire of Hades is arriving *before* we die, supposing we don't reverse global warming. Again, hell exists because we let it, but also, hell exists on earth because we create it.

Yet, here's the thing about time and our existence in this life and the afterlife: if God is love *and* love never ends, then forever has already begun. The clock for eternity starts before this earthly life ends, by the very definition of love! So whatever wondrous, merciful, reconciling love greets us at the heavenly gates is currently on offer. You don't have to wait until the *after* part of *life* to accept it. God doesn't need to do *after* because the God of love is now, then, and always. Christ reaffirmed God's reign of grace and expects it to grow through the good his followers pursue, banishing the hell-loops we live in and inflict on each other by demanding that love win now and for good.

In the final episode of *Lucifer*, "Partners Til the End," our charming hero comes to a major realization. He discovers a new purpose for himself within the whole of creation. After millennia of deep pain from being banished by Dad, then years of earthly therapy with Dr. Linda, and finally learning through loving Chloe to overcome his own self-loathing, Lucifer realizes that all the guilt that traps people in hell isn't forever; love is the only thing that never ends. His epiphany leads him to help several people escape their hell-loops. This surprises him almost as much as it surprises us; he enjoyed it! So he pivots his call to leadership from one of individual authority for personal satisfaction to one of collaboration for the sake of others.

Imagine that! The keeper of hell becomes its healer. But how? Through therapy of course! Obviously, Lucifer can't wave a wand and woosh people into glory. Hell exists because *we* let it. However, he can decorate a room in the underworld to look like his old therapist's office. Except now *he's* in the doctor's chair, prepared for an eternally therapeutic razing of hell, forever trying to liberate humanity from guilt.[80]

I love that ending because it honors the deepest truths I know about God and about love's forever longevity. It shows love's ability to outlast every limitation we've erected, every injustice we've inflicted, and every sin that trapped broken people in cycles of addiction, despair, abuse, hate, and greed. And if there's a real-life devil, I'm confident God's still trying to flip him back to the light because Love. Never. Ends. I love that ending...with one caveat.

Ever since hearing that medieval parable, I knew the story was incomplete. Remember Jesus' clearest statement on the afterlife? It's this: When you helped the suffering, the struggling, the oppressed, "you did it to me" (Mt. 25:40). Compassion welcomes us into paradise, and Jesus died demonstrating that sacrificial love.

So why then, in God's holy name, have so many Christians pretended love ends at our death? If there is a heavenly city with gnarled souls suffering outside its open gates, surely Jesus isn't gossiping from within, "Oooo, I know why he's that ashamed! Wanna know why she's so angry?" Hell no! He's rushing outside with fragrant bread, breaking it beneath tortured nostrils, whispering, "Taste and see. God is good!" Christ is outside the city walls offering a cup of resurrection to parched tongues, begging them to just look up, take a sip, and receive new life.

And, if you know Christ followers like I'm blessed to pastor, you know Christians wouldn't just watch Jesus work. These spiritual heroes would run behind, bellowing, "Savior, I'm coming too!"

If hell exists beyond earth, well, sorry Lucifer, but you weren't the first to give a damn about the damned. This life and the afterlife are filled with Christians sharing the unending love we have come to know. I am convinced that if there is a heavenly city, it is saturated with people of numerous faiths, surely, being and bearing the best of all news: God is love, and that love never ends, inside and outside the city walls. God's never-ending love beckons us, even when we don't—or can't—look up from our own guilt and shame.

And never means never: for me, for you, for Chloe, Lucifer, Dr. Linda, and even Reese too.

So, what are we to do with hell now? After all, the afterlife remains a mystery. All these paragraphs speculating what it could entail are simply that, speculation. However, we use fiction—TV, books, and parables—to tune in to what is happening and spark our holy imaginations into understanding more about the God we long to know more deeply. And I hope I've helped you find God and connect to a love so endless that you know no hell can exist forever. What's more, now I want to go to hell! I want to go so that I may be renewed in my spirit and be so blessed as to help Jesus (and maybe even Lucifer?)

break people out of their own entrapment. And if you share my conviction and I find myself trapped there, may you be there with Jesus, to come rescue and liberate me with God's eternal love.

But we don't know yet what is real on that side of the veil. On this side, however, in our cities and countrysides, with our divided neighbors, warming planet, addicted families, unequal communities, and our self-satisfying navel-gazing postures in the face of personal and systemic sin—hell on earth pervades. It traps too many of God's beloved children in cycles of sin and shame, injustice, and needless pain: "Truly I tell you, just as you did it to one of the least of these who are members of my family, you did it to me." (Mt. 25:40).

Jesus lives among us, urging the suffering to know they're not abandoned, begging the world to understand liberation is not only possible but present, and demanding his followers break whatever chains, whatever cycles, whatever hell-loops they see. Hell exists because we let it, but with God's endless love, we have the power to change it. Maybe that will be true after we die too, but that is no reason to wait.

Reflection Questions:

- If hell is not permanent, what is the point of sin?

- If heaven is always accessible, what is the point of sin?

- Considering God is love, love is always, and thus God is always, what can the Church learn from this about how we spend our time?

- If the devil can be redeemed, who in your life can be, too?

Chapter Twelve

Chaos as Virtue: Lessons from Loki on Mystery and Mischief

The Reverend Whitney Waller

Order is overrated.

Be honest, did reading that sentence make you cringe? I get it. Writing it felt a little weird too, but also right.

I used to believe an anal-retentive disposition, a good organizational system, and a well-articulated five-year plan were the holy trinity for my success and sanity, both professionally and personally. This belief has undergone some revision while co-existing with a two-year-old tornado who can make a mess from thin air and living through a pandemic that completely upended any sense of order or certainty. For my waking, mothering hours, the bulk of my time is spent building a future into existence for the little human who relies upon me to make today wonderful and tomorrow possible. During my child's (fewer than I would like) sleeping and resting hours, I try my best not to doom-scroll social media or gorge on news articles because it does indeed feel as though I am watching the world around me erode into a catastrophic mess. And, somewhere in the midst of all that, I also work full-time as a pastor, trying my best to proclaim a word of good news to people who are in need of some holy hope to make today bearable and tomorrow better.

As it turns out, when the world feels uncertain and unfamiliar, you begin to feel less compelled to create five-year plans. When every meeting is now prefaced with "tentative" and no longer requires leaving your house or changing out of pajama pants, your color-coded calendar does not really provide the same sense of comfort it once did. If your child can dirty plates and destroy rooms faster than you can clean them, you begin to question whether containing the mess is a worthwhile use of time. And, yes, I do mean the mess that extends beyond our kitchen sink and seems to seep into so many corners of our life.

What *does* feel like a worthwhile use of time when you're trying to manage your expectations in a far less structured and sane world than the one you thought you were living in?

Well, I think the answer is obvious. The best use of one's time in these circumstances is, of course, to consume as many apocalyptic stories as possible. I am sure this choice of comfort viewing and reading began as an exercise in *schadenfreude* meets escapism. I figured, if the world around me feels overwhelming and disorienting, I am sure I will feel better if I immerse myself in worlds that are even more overwhelming and disorienting. Because nothing makes you feel better than thinking that it could be worse, then exploring dozens of scenarios that are, indeed, worse than your current context. While it may feel counterintuitive for some, I did find that I felt better after reading a couple of chapters from *Leave the World Behind*. The chaos and uncertainty of my own life felt more manageable after binge-watching a few episodes of *Handmaid's Tale*.

At some point, however, during this apocalyptic project, the stated objective—to escape the difficulty of my present reality—shifted. I realized that my consumption was no longer fueled by a desire to know that things could be worse. Rather, I was inspired by the capacity for tenacity and transformation that people exhibited in worlds that were chaotic and crumbling.

This realization struck me while watching Season 1, Episode 4 of *Loki*, "The Nexus Event." In this Marvel Studios television series on Disney+, the God of Mischief himself, discovers he is not only himself. Avengers-adjacent Loki, played by Tom Hiddleston, is one of many iterations (known as variants) of Loki. Each of these variants exist in a different timeline, determined and delineated by a carefully calibrated calculus intended to maximize stability and order and minimize calamity and chaos within the Sacred Timeline, which holds together the many universes (the multiverse, if you will) that exist. If at any point a being acts beyond the bounds of their designated timeline, they are arrested by the Time Variance Authority (TVA) and charged accordingly. The TVA is initially presented as a necessary, upstanding bureaucratic organization tasked with preserving multiversal peace by bringing time criminals to justice. As viewers, we are led to believe that the TVA must apprehend and punish variants when they disrupt their timeline because any deviation from the intended timeline threatens to destroy the world. However, episode by episode the benevolent and beneficial role of the TVA within the multiverse becomes more and more suspect.

As we tune in to Episode 4, variants and viewers alike wonder how high the cost of preserving stability and order should be if it requires erasing entire populations and uprooting the lives of innocent people. In Episode 1, we are introduced by reputation to another Loki variant that the TVA is trying to capture. She has eluded the TVA for decades, but with the help of Hiddleston's Loki, this Goddess of Mischief has finally been located. While Hiddleston's Loki initially hoped that helping catch this variant might guarantee a more lenient sentence regarding his own crimes against the TVA, he becomes intrigued by the information and perspective this female version of himself, who goes by Sylvie, has to offer.

Sylvie confides in Loki about her past and why she has spent almost her entire life as a fugitive within the Sacred Timeline, outrunning and outsmarting the TVA:

> I remember Asgard. Not much, but I remember. My home, my people, my life. The universe wants to break free, so it manifests chaos. Like me being born the Goddess of Mischief. And as soon as that created a big enough detour from the Sacred Timeline, the TVA showed up, erased my reality, and took me prisoner. I was just a child.[81]

In sharing about her past, Sylvie reveals a painful truth: there is nothing sacred about this alleged timeline. The TVA does not exist to maintain order or preserve peace for the people of the multiverse. The TVA exists to preserve power for the select few who benefit from a world that can never be organic, spontaneous, or chaotic. The powers that be manipulate time so that they can create a false sense of order and stability. Sylvie, and now Loki, too, see through the façade of security and safety that the Sacred Timeline alleges to provide, and they realize they must dismantle the Sacred Timeline to free all beings from an existence that is inherently oppressive. Within the confines of the Sacred Timeline, no being can thrive or flourish because they cannot live into the fullness of their power or potential, for fear of disrupting the established order that allows for no meandering, mystery, or mischief.

No wonder the multiverse needs a couple mischief makers of god and goddess proportions to shake things up, challenge the status quo, and bring some chaos to a world desperate for a shock to its system. In the aftermath of discovering that two

Loki variants are working together to dismantle the Sacred Timeline, Mobius, a sympathetic TVA agent, remarks:

It's the apocalypse. Two variants of the same being, especially you, forming this kind of sick, twisted, romantic relationship. That's pure chaos. That could break reality. It's breaking my reality right now.[82]

Mobius, ultimately, realizes that reality is worth breaking and chaos is worth enduring because after this world splinters into disorder and uncertainty, something new might come to life, dare we say resurrect, amid the mystery and mischief.

The danger of making stability and demanding order from our gods is not only a plot point within the fictional multiverse, but also a theological conundrum present throughout scripture. This is an idea that is addressed with painstaking clarity in Revelation, another apocalyptic story we can find some comfort in—if we're looking for it!

Before it was a book in our Bibles, Revelation was a letter written to a community of early Christians struggling to live their faith audaciously and authentically under the rule of the Roman Empire. These Christians were required to proclaim, *"Caesar is Lord"* in word and deed. This declaration of Caesar's lordship was intended to serve as an acknowledgement of the Roman Emperor as their source of life, security, and peace. By requiring individuals to express their fidelity to and faith in Caesar's power, the Roman Empire sought to create compliance, stability, and order in new territories that they conquered. Declaring "Caesar is Lord" created a major conflict of interest for Christians who believe *"Jesus Christ is Lord"* and would consider it a betrayal of their God—who is their source of life, security, and peace—to say otherwise. This conflict of interest led to persecution, violence, and death for many Christians who refused to succumb to the statutes of the empire for the sake of preserving the version of *life, security, and peace* that Caesar's empire ordered.

As Rob Bell observes, Caesar's attempt to maintain order is hardly positive or peaceful for the everyday people who are usually hurt and rarely helped by the empire:

> It's only peace if you're holding the sword; to all those who were conquered by this devastating war machine— and hung on crosses—it wasn't peace.
>
> It was awful.
> It was oppressive.
> It was evil.[83]

In the throes of struggling to survive in this awful, oppressive, and evil world, someone wrote the letter we now know as Revelation. The letter was written to an early Christian community to provide them with a message of hope. The dear ones who would receive, read, hear, and heed this letter had been alienated and abused by the powers that be. To preserve his power, Caesar sought to establish dominance over anyone and everyone who might threaten to disrupt his law-and-order approach to ruling—such as those who may understand disrupting the unjust established powers as their sacred duty—a God of Mischief or Messiah, perhaps?

Revelation can be a difficult book to read. It is full of vivid, violent imagery that paints a messy, disordered, and chaotic view of what God's action looks like in our world. Our more contemporary interpretations of Revelation have overstated this use of imagery as some prophetic prediction of the future. In doing so, we fail to focus on the poetic, metaphorical function of the text that is, itself, transcendent and transformative for God's people. The author of Revelation describes scenes that shock and scare us in their apocalyptic nature to stir us from complacency and compliance. The shock value of this letter is not intended to elicit fear and a desire to cling to order in this world. The shock value of this letter is intended to encourage faith in a God whose mystery and mercy are only more expansive in the world to come.

On the other side of calamity, there is creation:

Then I saw a new heaven and a new earth;
for the first heaven and the first earth had passed away,
and the sea was no more. And I saw the holy city, the
new Jerusalem,
coming down out of heaven from God, prepared as a
bride adorned for her husband. And I heard a loud voice
from the throne saying,
"See, the home of God is among mortals.
He will dwell with them as their God;
they will be his peoples,
and God himself will be with them;
he will wipe every tear from their eyes.
Death will be no more;
mourning and crying and pain will be no more,
for the first things have passed away."
(Revelation 21:1–4)

Chaos is not typically the source of our calm, comfort, or control. In fact, we regularly feel as though chaos robs us of any sense of these. These are feelings we far more often associate with order. We like the idea of stability, because it feels like a guarantee of steadiness, safety, and steadfastness. Chaos feels like calamity, confusion, and complete disorder. Stability is good. Chaos is bad. And yet, we have seen—in compelling fiction, in composite stories of faith, and even in our own lived experience—that the roles of chaos and order are far more complicated and nuanced.

Order for the sake of order does not serve or save us. Often, order for the sake of order enslaves us unto the agendas, expectations, and desires of someone or something with no interest in our human flourishing or thriving. We want to think of our God as a God who prizes order, calm, and control. However, that doesn't exactly sound like the God we hear described in scripture, the Jesus we profess to follow, or the Holy Spirit that continues to help us discern, dream, and even disrupt. When we expect our lives to be free of mystery, mess, and uncertainty, we remove many potential opportunities for God to be at work. Our God is a God who values the miracles we find in the mystery, even when (and maybe especially when) life feels disordered.

If we could get more comfortable living in what singer Kevin Devine calls "the constant, bracing shock of now,"[84] we might find ourselves a little more at home, in ourselves and our world, even when we feel turned inside out. The timelines we create are not really all that sacred; they just make us feel like we have a little more control. So, maybe chaos has a sacred place in our lives as it calls us to reexamine and reimagine how we have ordered our lives to serve the heads of empires instead of the heart of God. What if our human chaos could serve as a conduit for the sacred mischievousness of the Holy Spirit, to disrupt unjust power for the sake of God's in-breaking love, and together create the church anew, not just for us—but *with* us.

Reflection Questions:

- How have you found your perceptions of order and chaos changed or challenged over the years?

- What is a biblical story that reminds you of how God is at work in the chaos of our lives?

- What do you see as the relationship between the Holy Spirit and the God of Mischief?

- How might you let the God of Mischief disrupt your status quo?

- What would a new heaven and a new earth look like for you?

Afterword

Keep Watching

Two On One Project, the podcast hosted by the co-editors of this book, is a "spoilers show," which is good, because so is the Bible. As faith leaders within the Christian tradition, we know how the show ends—at least how it is written—and have no problem telling you. The thing is, though, Jesus does not spend a lot of time dwelling on the end, and taking our cue from him, neither does *Two On One Project*. Sure, we'll talk about a series or season finale; sure, Jesus talks about when he is gone, but the bulk of our (Jesus and *Two On One Project's*) time is spent in conversation and reflection about the little stories that make up the larger one. That is why we intentionally end each episode of *Two On One Project* with the same question: What biblical person, book, theme, chapter, or verse are you most reminded of in the topic? This is our pivotal question because, while we all may be watching the same larger story arc, no show, story, book, or movie at its heart is just *one* story. Yes, we are people of the resurrection, but, as we have seen in these essays, we are also a part of the stories of the magi, the table, the disciples, and the kin-dom of each other.

That is why we hope you tune in every week to *Two On One Project*, but also to each other. We hope you are tuning in and are still watching, still hoping, and still curious about the stories we are living with God. It feels a little bit funny sometimes to ask our guests where they tune in to see God at work. More than once, we have had to reassure our guests that any movie or TV show that they are passionate about, no matter how seemingly random, bad, or banal, is ever void of the work of God—and we have yet to be proven wrong. That is because God can and does use everything in creation to connect with us and get us to connect with each other. It is no spoiler that relationships, community, and sharing our stories are the only way that we will get renewed for another season of ministry.

However, we have learned a lot about ministry, life, renewal, and what God is up to in these three seasons of *Two On One Project*, and so we want to offer you one spoiler of our own: You, the church, or as Spiff often says, "all the thing," have already been renewed. What we mean by that is that God, the great keeper of the ratings, has been tuning into the show of your life and always presses "Keep Watching." Yet in the world of film production, like in the world of church, the effort it takes to put on next season can be lessened if you have the right team, and luckily God is your showrunner.

Now, we can't say that just because we are all renewed, and God is running the show, that the work will be the same for each of us. Next season for you may not be easy or fair. There will be privilege and systemic oppression to fight. You may even find yourself in unique circumstances that feel lonely, or maybe even too hard. But as Coach Ted Lasso says in the finale of Season 1, "If God wanted games to end in a tie, She wouldn't have invented numbers,"[85] and your ratings are always Number 1 because God is running your show, and God's beloved community is your biggest fan. When we tune in to what is happening in this world and find God at work in ways we would have never expected, it supports the work we are called to do and reminds us that renewal can take many shapes. Your renewal may come in the form of a second season or a final season, it may come in the form of an extended break between seasons, it may even come in something unexpected like a spinoff, but you have been renewed through grace, and we are all excited as to what happens next.

This book was made in partnership with The Bethany Fellows, which is a leadership cohort for young clergy early in their vocational calling that strives to create in them good practices and strong community support so that, as ministers, they might creatively and savvily lead the church this season and the next. As with television, rarely do ministers and their churches avoid some sort of second-season slump, but Bethany Fellows' rhythm helps each Fellow strengthen their tools for best practices in their communities, so that the promise of renewal, either personal, communal, or spiritual, doesn't seem so unlikely when you have a challenging episode or even a bad season.

Each of our contributing authors are current participants or alumni of the Bethany Fellows, and they accepted the invitation to contribute right before Advent amidst multiple pandemics in our nation and world, all while holding in tension the incredible joys and challenges of being called to this vocation.[86] Thank you, Daniel, Colton, Rae, Travis, Larry, Jason, Diane, Delesslyn, Shane and Whitney.

So, are you still watching? We hope so! We hope that this book has helped you better understand that no matter what you are watching or hearing, all stories, if you tune in with intention, tell the story of God at work in the world. Whether you are watching for fun, rest, or inspiration, from the first episode to the end credits, God is at work, and your renewal is a guarantee—the renewal that is the eternal life found in the life, death, and resurrection of your beloved showrunner, Jesus. So when your pilot starts with energy and vision, and every episode after that has its joys and challenges no matter what you do, you can rest assured that when our time comes for the finale, when we come to the end of the album, or when the credits stop scrolling and the screen fades to black, we still get to live on in the eternal grace of God's syndication and streaming.

So cheers to this season you have worked so hard on, and may we all continue to tune in to God and each other and get renewed for whatever comes next.

Contributors

The Reverend Diane Faires Beadle (she/her) enjoys running, hiking, biking, cooking spicy foods, and making her community a more welcoming place for refugees, immigrants, and people of all religions. Before becoming an ordained pastor in the Christian Church (Disciples of Christ), Diane built houses with Habitat for Humanity and taught English in Sri Lanka. She is co-editor of *Acting on Faith: Stories of Courage, Activism and Hope Across Religions*. She is a graduate of Vanderbilt Divinity School and Rhodes College.

The Reverend Shane Isner (he/him) is a church pastor from Colorado who's followed a call to preach and teach through Chicago to the Upper Midwest, the Deep South, and other places between. His wife Tabitha—also ordained—practices progressive politics alongside business. Together, they raise a son, Tymari. Shane has served on numerous non-profit boards, published several writings, and can often be found coaching competitive soccer (USSF "D" License, USC Advanced National, so far...) or running long distances.

The Reverend Rae Karim (she/her) is a thought leader with a gift of words who pours lived experience into her work. This gift allows her to be a best-selling author and sought-after writer and speaker. She is also a two-time history maker, as the first woman and person of color to pastor non-Black churches in Indianapolis, Indiana and Honolulu, Hawaii. In all she does, Rae empowers and transforms lives, committed to ensuring she ignites courage on purpose for purpose.

The Reverend Stephanie Kendell (She/Elle/Ella) was born and raised in California but now comes to you "Live from New York..." where she serves in congregational and general church ministry with the Christian Church (Disciples of Christ). She is part of numerous justice-seeking organizations and ministries and co-hosts the *Two On One Project* podcast. Spiff has big dreams and even bigger cats, Physics and The Funk. She votes for justice and equity, hopes for sustainable peace and expansive love, and promotes God and all that She is doing in creation.

The Reverend Dr. Delesslyn A. Kennebrew (she/her) is a visionary strategist, inspirational essayist, and an ordained pastor in the Christian Church (Disciples of Christ). She uses innovation, strategic planning, and her wide breadth of experience, wisdom, and knowledge to guide the church through discerning, discovering, and developing what's next. Delesslyn prioritizes the work of transformation in all that she does, and her daily mantra is to BE EXCELLENT in what she thinks, speaks, and does.

The Reverend Colton D. Lott (he/him) is an ordained minister in the Christian Church (Disciples of Christ). He is from Ada, Oklahoma, the headquarters of the Chickasaw Nation, and makes an intergenerational home with his grandparents in El Reno, Oklahoma, where he serves in congregational ministry. Colton likes fountain pens, black tea, reading on his front porch, and his rescue dog, Babs.

The Reverend Daniel Lyvers (he/him) is an ordained minister in the Christian Church (Disciples of Christ) and feels particularly called to the work of love, hospitality, and community that derives from being around a table. Daniel loves being outside with his brindle hound dog, Chloe, playing around on the banjo, listening to the Avett Brothers, and all things Kentucky—particularly the basketball, the bourbon, and Wendell Berry.

The Reverend Travis Smith McKee (he/him) is a pastoral minister in the Christian Church in Kansas. He loves getting to talk about music, TV shows, and the future of the church. Travis aspires to be the Leslie Knope of his community, finding the grace of working together to accomplish meaningful things. He is a guitar player, at-home barista, and enjoys time outdoors with his family. Follow him on Twitter, @mckeetr22.

The Reverend Larry J. Morris III (he/they) is an apostle, digital marketer, scholar, and spiritual director based out of Henderson, Nevada. Larry has dedicated his life to God and the inclusive work of justice. Larry earned his master of divinity and master of theological studies degrees at Claremont School of Theology and, at the time of this writing, he's pursuing his Ph.D. in African American preaching and sacred rhetoric at Christian Theological Seminary.

The Reverend Jason Reynolds (he/him) is a Baptist pastor currently living and serving in San Jose, California. He is an agent of revitalization and renovation in congregational ministry, seeking to engage, grow, and reenergize the church. He is a faith leader in his community, an advocate for justice and equity for communities of color, an adjunct professor of philosophy, the producer of numerous films and theatrical plays, happily married to Poch'e, and the proud father of two sons, Jadon and Jason Reynolds II (affectionately called "Bubba").

The Reverend Arthur Stewart (he/him) is an ordained minister in the Christian Church (Disciples of Christ), a Bethany Ecumenical Fellow alumnus, and co-host of the *Two On One Project*. Arthur enjoys baking pies, improvisational storytelling, and deconstructing spy movies. In a previous life, he was a jazz musician and professional comedian. He and his husband, Brian, live in Wichita, Kansas with their daughter, Kenzie.

The Reverend Whitney Waller (she/her) is a professional extrovert, part-time theologian, and amateur polymath. An unapologetic enneagram 8, she spends (too) much of her time explaining to people, "I'm not angry, just passionate." Whitney channels her passion into her roles as mother, pastor, and friend. For Whitney, pop culture is a source of both inspiration and exasperation that reveals our human need to create and connect.

Endnotes

Introduction

[1]*The Office*, Season 5, Episode 23, "The Michael Scott Paper Company," directed by Gene Stupnitsky, written by Justin Spitzer, NBC, aired April 9, 2009.

Chaper One: *FOLLOWING A GLEAMING STAR*

[2]The Avett Brothers, "The Third Gleam: Announcement Video," YouTube, July 1, 2020, video, 3:14, https://www.youtube.com/watch?v=8KkKannG6AU.

[3]For an overview of the life, career, and music of the Avett Brothers, watch the documentary, *May It Last: A Portrait of the Avett Brothers*, directed by Judd Apatow and Michael Bonfiglio. Oscilloscope Laboratories, 2017.

[4]The Avett Brothers, "Back into the Light," track 4 on *The Third Gleam*, Loma Vista Recordings, 2020.

[5]Barbara Brown Taylor, "Home By Another Way," in *Home By Another Way* (Chicago: Rowman and Littlefield Publishing, 1999), Kindle e-book.

[6]Amy-Jill Levine, *Light of the World: A Beginner's Guide to Advent* (Nashville: Abingdon Press, 2019), 127.

[7]Amy-Jill Levine, *Light of the World*, 134.

[8]Colin Dwyer, "Jupiter and Saturn Will Be Together Again for the Holidays," December 9, 2020, *NPR*, https://www.npr.org/2020/12/09/944560103/jupiter-and-saturn-will-be-together-again-for-the-holidays.

[9]Amy-Jill Levine, *Light of the World,*130.

[10]The Avett Brothers, "Laundry Room," track 8 on *I and Love and You*, American Recordings, 2009.

[11]The Avett Brothers, "Murder in the City," track 2 on *The Second Gleam*, Ramseur Records, 2008.

[12]Dax Shephard and Monica Padman, "The Avett Brothers," September 30, 2019, *Armchair Expert*, podcast audio.

[13]The Avett Brothers, "The Once and Future Carpenter," track 1 on *The Carpenter,* American Recordings, 2012.

[14]The Avett Brothers, "Salvation Song," track 18 on *Mignonette,* Ramseur Records, 2004.

[15]*May It Last: A Portrait of the Avett Brothers,* directed by Judd Apatow and Michael Bonfiglio (Oscilloscope Laboratories, 2017).

[16]The Avett Brothers, "Fisher Road to Hollywood," track 9 on *True Sadness,* American Republic, 2016.

[17]The Avett Brothers, "Living of Love," track 10 on *Emotionalism,* Ramseur Records, 2007.

Chaper Two: *LET YOUR LIGHT SHINE*

[18]I must also mention that our society teaches us both misogyny and generalized mother-hating, and as a cisgender straight man, I am especially susceptible to both of these insidious notions.

[19]For more information on adult children of alcoholics, please visit https://adultchildren.org.

[20]Jennifer Damiano, Alice Ripley, et al., "Just Another Day," 2009, track 2 of disc 1 on *Next to Normal (Original Broadway Cast),* Ghostlight Records Inc., MP3.

[21]J. Robert Spencer, "He's Not Here," 2009, track 8 of disc 1 on *Next to Normal (Original Broadway Cast),* Ghostlight Records Inc., MP3.

[22]Jennifer Damiano, Lois Hobson, et al., "Who's Crazy/My Psychopharmacologist and I," 2009, track 4 of disc 1 on *Next to Normal (Original Broadway Cast),* Ghostlight Records Inc., MP3.

[23]Jennifer Damiano, Alice Ripley, and Aaron Tveit, "Superboy and the Invisible Girl," 2009, track 11 of disc 1 on *Next to Normal (Original Broadway Cast),* Ghostlight Records Inc., MP3.

[24]It is worth remembering that this is the gospel of Matthew's presentation of Jesus' life and thoughts. The historicity of this sermon in its present form, length, and content is up for considerable debate—and that debate is beyond the scope of this essay. Nevertheless, the gospel retained by the church presents this particularly influential set of teachings in this way, and it is from this vantage point that we begin to engage this text.

[25]Jennifer Damiano, Louis Hobson, et al., "Better Than Before," track 5 of disc 2 of *Next to Normal (Original Broadway Cast),* Ghostlight Records Inc., MP3.

[26]It's impossible to talk about *Next to Normal* without mentioning that it is a controversial show because of how it presents mental illness and mental health care. While it tells the story of one family's experience, it is (at best) ambivalent or (at worst) hostile about the effectiveness of mental health care for this fictious family. Our interpretations of art often affect the way we perceive our daily lives; in this case, *Next to Normal* can alter our perception of the role of mental health care and the efficacy of the treatments shown.

For more insight about the artistic presentation of mental illness and mental health care in *Next to Normal,* in context of the general history of mental illness represented on Broadway, please see Patricia Cohen, "Mental Illness, the Musical, Aims for Truth," *The New York Times,* April 16, 2009, accessed December 31, 2021, https://www.nytimes.com/2009/04/19/theater/19cohe.html.

For insight from a former electroconvulsive therapy (ECT) patient about how the experience and efficacy of ECT is portrayed in *Next to Normal,* please see Julie K Hersh, "Is 'Next to Normal' Normal?" Psychology Today (blog), June 19, 2010, accessed December 31, 2021, https://www.psychologytoday.com/us/blog/struck-living/201006/is-next-normal-normal.

[27]Jennifer Damiano and Alice Ripley, "Maybe (Next to Normal)," 2009, track 15 of disc 2 on *Next to Normal (Original Broadway Cast)*, Ghostlight Records Inc., MP3.

[28]Ibid.

[29]Ibid.

[30]Ibid.

[31]Alice Ripley and J. Robert Spencer, "A Light in the Dark," track 18 of disc 1 on *Next to Normal (Original Broadway Cast)*, Ghostlight Records Inc., MP3.

[32]Jennifer Damiano, Alice Ripley, et al., "Light," track 19 of disc 2 on *Next to Normal (Original Broadway Cast)*, Ghostlight Records Inc., MP3.

[33]Ibid.

Chaper Three: *LET YOUR LIGHT SHINE: BARBECUE SAUCE*

34*Ted Lasso*, Season 1, Episode 8, "The Diamond Dogs," directed by Declan Lowney, w. Written by Jason Sudeikis, Bill Lawrence, and Brendan Hunt,. Apple TV+, September. 18, 2020.

35Ibid.

36I am using "win" as an analogy for salvation/building the kin-dom.

37*Ted Lasso*, Season 1, Episode 3, "Trent Crimm: The Independent," directed by Tom Marshall, written by Jason Sudeikis, Bill Lawrence, and Brendan Hunt, Apple TV+, August 14, 2020.

Chaper Four: *FORGET WHAT'S BEHIND*

38*The Harder They Fall*, directed by Jeymes Samuel, Overbrook Entertainment, 2021, Netflix.

39It is a fantastic online resource; check out www.blueletterbible.org.

Chaper Five: *LORD, ONLY YOU CAN ANSWER THAT*

40"The Beatles: Get Back," *Day 7*, directed By Peter Jackson, 1hr 03min, Disney+.

41Peter Jackson, "Peter Jackson Reveals How He Convinced Beatles Paul and Ringo To Let Him Make 'Get Back'" interviewed by Variety, Youtube video, 1:45, November 26, 2021, https://www.youtube.com/watch?v=K95MIzDth_A.

42Peter Jackson, "Peter Jackson Reveals How He Convinced Beatles Paul and Ringo To Let Him Make 'Get Back'" interviewed by Variety, Youtube video, 0:03, November 26, 2021, https://www.youtube.com/watch?v=K95MIzDth_A.

Chaper Six: *THE SUN HAS GAZED ON ME*

43Renita Weems, "The Song of Songs," in *The New Interpreter's Bible: A Commentary in Twelve Volumes,* volume V, (Nashville: Abingdon Press, 1998) 363.

44Ibid. The book of Esther is the only other biblical book that does not explicitly name God.

45Ibid., 364.

46Ibid., 364.

[47]*Dictionary by Merriam-Webster*, s.v. "decolonize," accessed December 12, 2021, https://www.merriam-webster.com/dictionary/decolonize.

[48]Stephanie Pappas and Callum McKelvie, "What Is Culture?," Live Science, December 15, 2021, https://www.livescience.com/21478-what-is-culture-definition-of-culture.html.

[49]Trevor Anderson, "Beyoncé Ties Michael Jackson's Top 40 Mark as 'Black Parade' Debuts on Billboard Hot 100," Billboard, July 3, 2020, https://www.billboard.com/pro/beyonce-black-parade-michael-jackson-top-40-hot-100-hits/.

[50]Gary Trust, "Dababy & Roddy Ricch's 'Rockstar' Returns to No. 1 on Hot 100, Jack Harlow & Lil Mosey Earn Their First Top 10s," Billboard, June 29, 2020, https://www.billboard.com/pro/dababy-rockstar-number-one-hot-100-third-week/.

[51]Rhian Daly, "Beyoncé Breaks Record for Most Grammy Wins for a Female Artist and Any Singer," NME, March 15, 2021, https://www.nme.com/news/music/beyonce-breaks-record-most-grammy-wins-female-artist-any-singer-2900414.

[52]Jeffries, B. S., s.v. "Oshun," *Encyclopedia Britannica*, September 3, 2017, https://www.britannica.com/topic/Oshun.

[53]Canson, P. E., s.v. "Yemonja," *Encyclopedia Britannica*, August 15, 2014, https://www.britannica.com/topic/Yemonja.

Chaper Seven: *THE TOWN WHERE I CURRENTLY AM*

[54]Katie Hays, *God Gets Everything God Wants* (Grand Rapids, MI: Eerdmans, 2021).

[55]Isasi-Díaz, Ana Maria, *Mujerista Theology* (Maryknoll, NY: Orbis Books, 1996) 89–90.

[56]*Schitts Creek*, season 4, "Breaking Good," YouTube video, 1:47, December 25, 2017, https://youtu.be/90HRhq84NYw.

[57]You may notice that the subtitle includes the phrase "get renewed for another season." Yes, that is a television-industry reference! Yes, that points to the weird, inescapable, and never-ending pandemic we're all stuck in. Yes, that points to our liturgical year and the long haul of showing up for one another week in and week out. It is an inclusive phrase!

[58]One could argue that there are other glimpses of the kin-dom of God prior to the second season finale of Schitt's Creek. I accept that, and bless it—for me, this is a turning point in the show.

[59]*I'm not the least bit sorry.*

[60]*Schitt's Creek*, "Happy Anniversary," directed by Paul Fox, written by Dan Levy and Eugene Levy, Pop TV, March 29, 2016.

[61]Ibid.

[62]I don't know if you know this, but I'm doing a study on the letters of the apostle Paul. I have mentioned this with alarming frequency on *Two On One Project*. I would be remiss not to do so in a footnote!

[63]*Schitt's Creek*, "Happy Anniversary," directed by Paul Fox, written by Dan Levy and Eugene Levy, Pop TV, March 29, 2016.

[64]Dictionary.com, s.v. "pansexual," accessed January 5, 2022, https://www.dictionary.com/e/gender-sexuality/pansexual/.

[65]*Schitt's Creek*, "Honeymoon," directed by Jerry Ciccoritti, written by Dan Levy and Eugene Levy, Pop TV, April 15, 2015.

[66]Schitt's Creek (Youtube channel), "Cast Roundtable–Part 1," YouTube Video, 25:02, April 13, 2019, https://youtu.be/i2BMt5MoO5o.

Chaper Eight: *DO OUR CHOICES MATTER?*

[67]*Foundation*, episode 4, "Barbarians at the Gate," directed by Alex Graves, released October 8, 2021, Apple TV+.

[68]*Foundation*, episode 5, "Upon Awakening," directed by Alex Graves, released October 15, 2021, Apple TV+.

[69]"Foundation: Apple TV+," Apple TV, September 24, 2021, accessed November 1, 2021, https://tv.apple.com/us/show/foundation/umc.cmc.5983fipzqbicvrve6jdfep4x3.

[70]Big Sean, "One Man Can Change the World," track 11 on *Dark Sky Paradise (Deluxe)*, G.O.O.D. Music and Def Jam Recordings, 2015, Spotify.

[71]*Foundation*, episode 4, "Barbarians at the Gate," directed by Alex Graves, released October 8, 2021, Apple TV+.

Chaper Nine: *ONE BODY, MANY MEMBERS*

[72]A huge thanks to Eric C. Smith, *Paul the Progressive? The Compassionate Christian's Guide to Reclaiming the Apostle as an Ally* (Chalice Press, 2019), which I rely heavily on for this understanding of Paul's views on status and sexuality.

[73]Some examples of these passages include Romans 1:24–32, 1 Corinthians 6:9–11, 1 Timothy 1:8–11.

[74]*Queer Eye*, season 5, episode 1, "Preaching Out Loud," produced by Mark Bracero, David Collins, et. al, aired June 5, 2020, Netflix.

[75]Ibid.

Chaper Ten: *WHERE IS FAT JESUS?*

[76]"About the Show—My 600-Lb Life," TLC, accessed November 29, 2021, https://www.tlc.com/tv-shows/my-600-lb-life/about.

Chaper Eleven: *GO TO HELL, CHRISTIAN!*

[77]*Lucifer*, season 3, episode 7, "Off the Record," directed by Eduardo Sánchez, aired November 13, 2017, FOX.

[78]Ibid.

[79]Ibid.

[80]*Lucifer*, season 6, episode 10, "Partners 'Til the End," directed by Sherwin Shilati, aired September 10, 2021, Netflix.

Chaper Twelve: *CHAOS AS VIRTUE*

[81]*Loki,* season 1, episode 4, "Nexus Event," created by Michael Waldron, 2021, Disney+.

[82]Ibid.

[83]Rob Bell, *What Is the Bible? How an Ancient Library of Poems, Letters and Stories Can Transform the Way You Think and Feel About Everything* (New York: HarperCollins, 2017) 207, Kindle edition.

[84]Kevin Devine, "Another Bag of Bones," track 3 on *Brothers Blood*, Favorite Gentlemen, 2009.

AFTERWORD

[85] *Ted Lasso*, Season 1, Episode 10, "The Hope That Kills You," created by Jason Sudeikis, Bill Lawrence, et. al., 2020, Apple TV+.

[86] Arthur will insist there's only two seasons in the church: Advent and almost-Advent.